The Ultimate ~~BLONDE~~ Kamala Joke book

And other fun Stuff!

James Pace

AuthorJamesPace@yahoo.com

www.TheUltimateKamalaJokeBook.com

Published in 2024 by James Pace and illustrated by James Pace.
All rights reserved. No portion of this book may be reproduced,
stored in a retrieval system, or transmitted in any form or by
means, mechanical, electronic, photocopying, recording, or
otherwise, without written permission from the publisher. Please
contact Author JamesPace@yahoo.com for permission to use
materials from this book.
Thank you for supporting author's rights.

Dedication

This book to dedicate to:

To GOD, thank you for all things possible.

To My Dad in Heaven, thank you for being so damn funny!

To My Mom, thank you for giving birth to me.

To My Stepmom, thank you for all the joke books when I was a kid.

To My Wife, thank you for letting me be me.

To the rest of my family, thank you for your love and support through my life.

To My Son Michael, here is your joke in a book.

"What do you call a dog that looks like Kamala? - A Harris Dog"

Contents

Dedication--i

Kamala Jokes---2

Mommy Mommy Jokes------------------------------------40

Limericks---41

Quotes--45

Recipes---60

Desertss--77

Cocktails---84

Kamala Medical Terms---------------------------------88

Coloring pages--92

Word Find---105

The Declaration Of Independence------------------109

Constitution of the United States-------------------120

Patriotic Songs---138

Autographs---148

Notes---149

Publisher's Note:

The following content is a parody, created for entertainment purposes only. It is a fictional representation and should not be taken as factual. This work is in no way affiliated with, endorsed by, or representative of the original source material or its creators. Any similarities to real-life events, people, or organizations are coincidental and not intended to be taken as literal interpretations. This parody is not meant to defame or infringe upon the rights and reputations of any persons, living or deceased, or entities involved with the original work.

Kamala Jokes

1. How do you keep Kamala busy for hours? – Just place a mirror in front of her and have her play Rock, Paper, Scissors.

♦ ♦ ♦

2. What do you get when you give Kamala a penny for her thoughts? – Change

♦ ♦ ♦

3. Why is it easier to park with Kamala in the car? – You can park in a handicap space.

♦ ♦ ♦

4. Pelosi ask Kamala, "Do you believe there is life on the moon" – Of course there is, they have all their lights on.

♦ ♦ ♦

5. Why doesn't Kamala water ski? - Because she hasn't found a lake with a slope yet.

♦ ♦ ♦

6. AOC asked Kamala if she took a pregnancy test and Kalama said "yes, but the questions were really hard".

♦ ♦ ♦

7. Why can't you tell Kamala knock-knock jokes? – Because she always leaves to go answer the door.

8. Why did Kamala eat her food so fast? – She thought she was fasting.

♦ ♦ ♦

9. Why did Kamala put lipstick on her forehead? – To make up her mind.

♦ ♦ ♦

10. Why does Kamala never get headaches? – No brain no pain.

♦ ♦ ♦

11. What's the difference between a pregnant Kamala and a light bulb? – You can unscrew a light bulb.

♦ ♦ ♦

12. Why did Kamala bring a ladder to a bar? – They told her drinks were on the house.

♦ ♦ ♦

13. How do you confuse Kamala? - Tell her while in the oval office to sit in the corner.

♦ ♦ ♦

14. What do screen doors and Kamala have in common? – The more you use them, the looser they get.

♦ ♦ ♦

15. Why doesn't Kamala talk during sex? – Her mom taught her not to talk to strangers.

16. What did Kamala say when she found out she was pregnant? – I wonder if it's mine.

♦ ♦ ♦

17. Why did Kamala stare at the orange juice jug for hours? – Because it said concentrate.

♦ ♦ ♦

18. Why does Kamala love her boob job? – Because it's the only job she's qualified for.

♦ ♦ ♦

19. What did Kamala say after seeing a cheerios box? – Look donut seeds.

♦ ♦ ♦

20. What's Kamala's dream job? – To be like Vanna White and learn the alphabet.

♦ ♦ ♦

21. Why did Kamala get so excited about finishing the puzzle in 2 months? – Because the box said "2 to 4 years."

♦ ♦ ♦

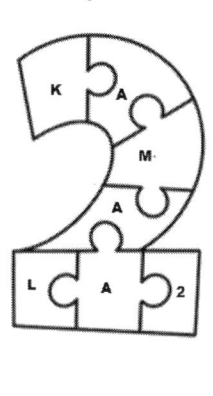

22. How do you keep Kamala in the shower all day? – Give her a bottle of shampoo that says "lather, rinse, and repeat."

♦ ♦ ♦

23. Kamala bought an AM radio but it took her months to figure out she could use it at night.

♦ ♦ ♦

24. Kamala: "What does IDK stand for?" AOC: "I don't know" Kamala: "OMG nobody knows."

♦ ♦ ♦

25. Kamala, AOC, and Pelosi walk into a building…. You would think at least one of them would have seen it.

♦ ♦ ♦

26. Kamala and AOC drove to Disneyworld and the sign said "Disneyworld Left." So they started crying and went back to DC.

27. Why isn't Kamala a good cattle herder? – Because she can't even keep two calves together.

♦ ♦ ♦

28. Why does Kamala dive a car with a sunroof? – More leg room.

♦ ♦ ♦

29. What's the difference between Kamala and a solar powered calculator? – Kamala works in the dark.

♦ ♦ ♦

30. Why did Kamala tip-toe past the medicine cabinet? She didn't want to wake up the sleeping pills.

♦ ♦ ♦

31. How to you keep Kamala home? – Build a circular driveway.

♦ ♦ ♦

32. How do you make Kamala's eyes light up? – Shine a light in her ears.

♦ ♦ ♦

33. Why are Kamala jokes so short? – So she can remember them.

♦ ♦ ♦

34. Why didn't Kamala and 18 of her friends go into a bar? – The sign said 21+.

35. How did Kamala's brain cell die? – Alone

♦ ♦ ♦

36. Why did Kamala climb on to the roof? - Because someone said the drinks are on the house.

♦ ♦ ♦

37. Why does Kamala drive a BMW? – Because she can spell it.

38. How did Kamala break her leg raking leaves? – She just fell out of a coconut tree.

♦ ♦ ♦

39. How do you make Kamala laugh on Sunday? – Tell her a joke on Wednesday.

♦ ♦ ♦

40. Why did Kamala clime the glass wall? - So she could she what was on the other side.

41. Why does it take longer to build a Kamala snowman? – Because you have to hollow out the head.

♦ ♦ ♦

42. Why couldn't Kamala write 11? – She couldn't figure out which number came first.

♦ ♦ ♦

43. AOC and Kamala fell down a hole. AOC said "It's dark in here" and Kamala said "I don't know, I can't see."

♦ ♦ ♦

44. Why couldn't Kamala add 10 and 7 on the calculator? – She couldn't find the 10 key.

♦ ♦ ♦

45. How do you keep Kamala busy? – Write "flip over" on both sides of the paper.

♦ ♦ ♦

46. Why does Kamala wear so much hairspray? – So she can catch all the things that go over her head.

♦ ♦ ♦

47. What's the difference between a smart version of Kamala and Bigfoot? – Bigfoot has actually been sighted.

48. Why does Kamala like lighting? – She thinks someone is taking her picture.

♦ ♦ ♦

49. Why did Kamala get fired from the M&M factory? – She kept throwing out all of the W's.

♦ ♦ ♦

50. Joe: Knock-knock? Kamala who's there? – Look who just fell out of the coconut tree?

♦ ♦ ♦

51. Kamala says she eats No for breakfast! What does Willy Brown have to ay on that subject?

♦ ♦ ♦

52. Why can't Kamala Dial 911? – She can't find the 11.

♦ ♦ ♦

53. Someone steals a TV from the store that cost less than $900.00 and Kamala runs after him and says, "Stop, you forgot the remote."

♦ ♦ ♦

54. What does Kamala put behind her ears to make her more attractive? - Her ankles.

♦ ♦ ♦

55. How do you know when Kamala has been using the computer? – There is whiteout on the screen.

♦ ♦ ♦

56. What do you call Kamala if she had 2 brain cells? – Pregnant.

♦ ♦ ♦

57. Why did Kamala bring a red marker to work? – In case she had to draw blood.

♦ ♦ ♦

58. Why should Kamala not get coffee breaks? – It takes too long to retrain her.

♦ ♦ ♦

59. What's the difference between Kamala and a computer? – You only have to enter information in the computer once.

♦ ♦ ♦

60. How can you tell when Kamala sends a fax? – There's a stamp on it.

♦ ♦ ♦

61. How did Kamala die drinking milk? – The cow fell on her.

♦ ♦ ♦

62. What do you get when you line up AOC, Kamala, Pelosi, Mad Max, and Omar side by side? – A wind tunnel.

♦ ♦ ♦

63. What's the first thing Kamala does in the morning? – Goes home.

♦ ♦ ♦

64. How can you tell if Kamala has been making chocolate chip cookies? – There are M&M shells all over the floor.

♦ ♦ ♦

65. To Kamala, what's long and hard? - 4th grade.

♦ ♦ ♦

66. Why did Kamala keep doing the backstroke? – She didn't want to swim on a full stomach.

♦ ♦ ♦

67. Why can't Kamala ever be vegan? – Because she's a turkey playing chicken in a beef over pork and that's a little fishy.

♦ ♦ ♦

68. What did Kamala order for dinner on Election night? – Stuffed ballots.

♦ ♦ ♦

69. What do you call a bad lawyer? – A Senator

♦ ♦ ♦

70. Why do thieves never target Kamala's house? – Professional courtesy.

71. Why can't you let Kamala on a plane? – Because she'll try to destroy the right wing.

72. A clown, Walz, and Harris walk in to a bar. And the bartender says "When did the circus get into town?"

73. A clown, a priest and Harris walk into a bar. The bartender says, "What is this some kind of a joke?"

74. Kamala can find an excuse to get out of anything . Except office.

♦ ♦ ♦

75. I was arrested for impersonating Kamala but all I was doing was sitting in my office doing nothing.

♦ ♦ ♦

76. Kamala is a person that will lay down your life for their country.

♦ ♦ ♦

77. When Kamala says she will stand on her record, she literally means it – to keep you from checking it.

♦ ♦ ♦

78. When I was a kid, my dad told me anyone could become president. As a grown-up Kamala becoming president gives me nightmares.

♦ ♦ ♦

79. "I will fix things if you vote me into office'" says Kamala who is currently in office.

♦ ♦ ♦

80. Twice the stupidity without the dementia! Harris 2024

♦ ♦ ♦

81. We don't approve of political jokes, especially if Kamala gets elected.

♦ ♦ ♦

82. What branch of the military did Walz belong to? -The Infantry

♦ ♦ ♦

83. There are two things I don't like about Kamala . . . her face!

♦ ♦ ♦

84. What was Walz's rank when he discharged? – General waste.

♦ ♦ ♦

85. Kamala should wear a uniform like NASCAR drivers so we can identify her corporate sponsors.

♦ ♦ ♦

86. What is the difference between Kamala and a snail? – One is slimy, a pest, and leaves a trail of waste and the other is a snail.

♦ ♦ ♦

87. What do you call a lawyer with the IQ of 120? – Your Honor

♦ ♦ ♦

88. What do you call a lawyer with an IQ of 50? - Senator Harris.

♦ ♦ ♦

89. Instead of giving Kamala the key to the country, it might be better to change the locks!

♦ ♦ ♦

90. What's the difference between Baseball and Kamala? – In baseball you're out if caught stealing.

♦ ♦ ♦

91. Why are Kamala jokes so short? – So liberals can remember them.

♦ ♦ ♦

92. How did Trump get Kamala out of the coconut tree? - He cut that damn thing down like Washington cutting down a cherry tree.

♦ ♦ ♦

93. How do you make Kamala's eyes light up? – Shine a flashlight in her ear.

♦ ♦ ♦

94. What is the new dance of 2024? - It's the Kamala Waltz, you just stand there look stupid and lie about being at the big dance.

♦ ♦ ♦

95. AOC and Kamala got lost at the mall. So they go to the map and find the red arrow that says "you are here". Harris says to AOC "WOW, How did they know that?"

♦ ♦ ♦

96. Kamala to her Doctor: "I swallowed an ice cube the other day at it still hasn't come out."

♦ ♦ ♦

97. Why did Kamala buy an elephant instead of a car? – She heard the elephant has a bigger trunk.

98. Why did Kamala hate to visit the Oval office with Biden? Every time Biden told her to sit in the corner and she got lost.

♦ ♦ ♦

99. Why did Kamala wear underwear in her twenties? – To keep her ankles warm.

♦ ♦ ♦

100. What can you do to confuse Kamala? – Nothing, she was born that way.

♦ ♦ ♦

101. Trump is the straw that broke the Camel toe's back.

♦ ♦ ♦

102. What is the definition of gross ignorance? – 144 liberals.

♦ ♦ ♦

103. How did the Navy drown Kamala on a Submarine? – The Knocked on the door.

♦ ♦ ♦

104. How is Kamala like a piano? - When she's not upright, she grand.

♦ ♦ ♦

105. What do Kamala and a beer bottle have in common? – They are both empty from the neck up.

♦ ♦ ♦

106. Kamala drops off her dress at the dry cleaners and the lady says, "Come again!" And Harris says, "No, it's toothpaste this time."

♦ ♦ ♦

107. Why does Kamala wear rubber gloves while typing on her computer? – She didn't want to catch a computer virus.

♦ ♦ ♦

108. What do you call 20 liberals in a freezer? –Frosted flakes.

♦ ♦ ♦

109. Did you hear that Kamala took up archery and shot the arrow into the air? –She missed.

♦ ♦ ♦

110. What do you call it when Walz whispers into Kamala's ear? – Data transfer

♦ ♦ ♦

111. Why do Liberals only want three children? – Because there heard from CNN that one in four children born is Chinese.

♦ ♦ ♦

112. Kamala asked AOC if she thinks Florida is farther away than the moon. – "What do you think stupid? Can you see Florida from here?"

♦ ♦ ♦

113. Biden to Harris, we went from pee pads to knee pads,

♦ ♦ ♦

114. Why did Kalama put her iPad in a blender? –She wanted to make apple juice.

♦ ♦ ♦

115. AOC: "Where were you born?" Kamala: "The United States." AOC: "Which part?" Kamala "My whole body."

♦ ♦ ♦

116. How can you tell Kamala is actually a blond? –When she trips over the cordless phone.

♦ ♦ ♦

117. Kamala calls Walz and says "What's your number? I can't find it."

♦ ♦ ♦

118. I man walks By Kamala, who is holding a pig. The man asks, "Where did you get her?" The pig answered, "I won her at the fair."

♦ ♦ ♦

119. How did Kamala die? – Someone put a scratch-and-sniff at the bottom of the pool.

♦ ♦ ♦

120. Why can't Kamala tie her own shoes? -Because she can't grasp the concept that the long thing goes around the hole, not into it.

♦ ♦ ♦

121. Kamala: "You ever smell moth balls?" AOC: "yes, I think they smell nice." Kamala: "Wow, I can't believe you got your nose between those tiny legs."

♦ ♦ ♦

122. Why did Kamala put water on her computer? – To wash the windows.

♦ ♦ ♦

123. Kamala asked her parents, "Why does my brother have two sisters and I only have one?"

124. What do Kamala and a dim light have in common? – They are both hot but not too bright.

♦ ♦ ♦

125. What is the difference between Kamala as president and a unicorn? - Nothing, they are both fictional.

♦ ♦ ♦

126. Why do liberals walk in groups of odd numbers? - Because they can't even.

♦ ♦ ♦

127. What were Kamala's first words after graduating college? - "Would you like fries with that?"

♦ ♦ ♦

128. Kamala crashed Marine one. The secret service asked her "what happened?" She says, "It got cold so I turned off the fan."

♦ ♦ ♦

129. How do you confuse Kamala? – Give her a box of corn flakes and tell her it's a puzzle.

♦ ♦ ♦

130. Why did Kamala pee on the floor? –Because she saw a sign that said "Wet floor."

♦ ♦ ♦

131. Why does Kamala have "TGIF written on her shoes? - To remind her that Toes Go In First.

♦ ♦ ♦

132. How many liberals does it take to screw in a light bulb? –Too many to count.

♦ ♦ ♦

133. Why were there bullet holes in the mirror? - Kamala tried to kill herself after losing to Trump.

♦ ♦ ♦

134. Why can't Kamala make Kool-Aid? – She can't fit 8 quarts of water into the tiny packet.

♦ ♦ ♦

135. How can you tell Kamala is having a bad day? – She can't find her pencil and her Tampon is behind her ear.

♦ ♦ ♦

136. Why does Kamala have empty beer can in her frig? - For her friends that don't drink.

♦ ♦ ♦

137. Why did Kamala return the puzzle? – It was broken.

♦ ♦ ♦

138. Why did Kamala have the biggest breast in the third grade? - Because she was 21.

139. What would you call Kamala if she had half a brain? – Gifted.

♦ ♦ ♦

140. What do Kamala and a door knob have in common? – Everyone gets a turn.

♦ ♦ ♦

141. Kamala making "Blonds look smart again"

♦ ♦ ♦

142. Why doesn't Kamala eat M&Ms? – Because they are too hard to peel.

♦ ♦ ♦

143. Did you hear how Kamala burnt her face while working at McDonalds? – She was bobbing for french fries.

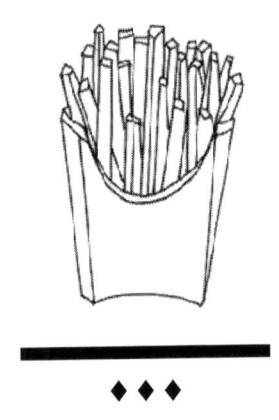

♦ ♦ ♦

144. What did Kamala's left leg say to her right leg? – Between the two of us we can make a lot of money.

♦ ♦ ♦

145. What is the difference between Biden and Kamala? – Kamala's sperm count is higher.

♦ ♦ ♦

146. How does Kamala spell farm? – E-I-E-I-O.

♦ ♦ ♦

147. Why did Kamala put sugar on her pillow? – She wanted to have sweet dreams.

♦ ♦ ♦

148. What did Kamala say When Biden blew in her ear? - Thanks for the refill.

♦ ♦ ♦

149. What's it called when one liberal blows into another liberal's ear? – A date transfer.

♦ ♦ ♦

150. How did Douglas get Kamala to marry him? – He told her she was pregnant.

♦ ♦ ♦

151. Why did Kamala snort Splenda? – She thought it was diet coke.

152. Kamala heard accidents happen close to home, so she moved.

♦ ♦ ♦

153. What do you call a mosquito flying in Kamala's head? – A Space invader.

♦ ♦ ♦

154. What can strike Kamala without her knowing it? – An original thought.

♦ ♦ ♦

155. What is the first thing Kamala does in the morning? - Introduces herself.

♦ ♦ ♦

156. What is Kamala's favorite fairy tale? – Humpme Dumpme.

♦ ♦ ♦

157. Why is 68 the max speed for Harris? - Because at 69 she blows a rod.

♦ ♦ ♦

158. Maybe if we tell Kamala the brain is in an App she'll start using it.

♦ ♦ ♦

159. Kamala's IQ came back negative.

♦ ♦ ♦

160. What is Kamala's idea of safe sex? – Lock the car door first.

♦ ♦ ♦

161. What does Kamala think about the math test? - Nothing.

♦ ♦ ♦

162. Why is it impossible for Kamala to make a funny joke? - Because she is the joke.

♦ ♦ ♦

163. Did you hear the Kalama and Tim were found frozen to death in their car at the drive-in movie theatre? - They apparently went to see "Closed for the winter."

♦ ♦ ♦

164. Kalama orders a pizza and the clerk asked if he should cut it into six, eight or twelve pieces. Kalama replies "Six please. I could never eat twelve".

♦ ♦ ♦

165. Kalama, AOC and a Pelosi were trapped on an island and the nearest land was 50 miles away. Pelosi swam towards land but only made it 15 miles then drowned. AOC swam 23 miles and then drowned. Kalama swam 25 miles but then got tired so swam back to the island.

♦ ♦ ♦

166. Did you hear that Kalama tried to blow up her husband's car? - She burnt her lips on the exhaust pipe.

♦ ♦ ♦

167. What is five miles long and has an IQ of 40? - A parade of Liberals.

♦ ♦ ♦

168. What does Kalama and dog poo have in common? - The older she gets, the easier she is to pick up.

♦ ♦ ♦

169. Why was Kalama's belly button sore? - Her husband was a liberal too.

♦ ♦ ♦

170. Kalama was getting sick of all the liberal jokes that she was hearing at work so one night she decided to go home and learn all of the state capitals of the US. She comes into work the next day and proudly claims, "We liberals are smarter than you realize, I know all of the state capitals, test me and I'll tell you the answer". A fellow worker says, "Ok, tell me what's the capital of Florida?" Kamala replies "F"

171. Kamala is standing on one side of the river when she sees AOC on the other side. She yells out to her "How do you get to the other side of the river?" AOC responds "don't be so stupid, you are already on the other side".

♦ ♦ ♦

172. What goes vroom, screech, vroom, and screech? - Kamala at a flashing red light.

♦ ♦ ♦

173. What does Kamala do when her laptop freezes? - Microwave it.

♦ ♦ ♦

174. What do you call a basement full of liberals? - A wine cellar.

♦ ♦ ♦

175. I asked Kamala why she kept empty beer bottles in the refrigerator. She said, "They're for my friends who don't drink."

♦ ♦ ♦

176. What did Kamala say to the buxom waitress when reading her name tag? "'Sarah'...that's cute. What did you name the other one?"

♦ ♦ ♦

177. Kamala walks into a hospital and claims that everywhere she touches hurts... The doctor says, "Ma'am, you have a broken finger."

♦ ♦ ♦

178. Did you hear about the near-tragedy at the mall? - There was a power outage and a dozen liberals were stuck on the escalators for more than four hours.

♦ ♦ ♦

179. .Kalama's password had to be eight characters long and include at least one capital. So she made it "BidenPelosiSchumerNadlerOmarTlaibWatersSander"

♦ ♦ ♦

180. What do the Bermuda Triangle and Kamala have in common? - They both swallow a lot of sea men.

♦ ♦ ♦

181. 19. What do you call a liberal with an actual brain? - Republican.

♦ ♦ ♦

182. Kamala and AOC are in an elevator. A guy gets in with really bad dandruff. AOC whispers "Someone should give the poor guy some Head and Shoulders." Kalama says "How do you give shoulders?"

♦ ♦ ♦

183. Why did Kamala put condoms on her ears? - To avoid getting hearing AIDS.

♦ ♦ ♦

184. What do you give Kamala since she has everything? - Penicillin.

♦ ♦ ♦

185. Kamala thought a quarterback was a refund.

♦ ♦ ♦

186. What is Kamala's psychic's greatest achievement? – An in-body experience.

♦ ♦ ♦

187. Kamala keeps a ruler in bed to measure how long she sleeps each night.

♦ ♦ ♦

188. What did Slick Willy say to his partner after sex with Kamala? - Hi honey, I'll be home in 30 minutes.

♦ ♦ ♦

189. Why was Kamala sad when she looked at her driver's license? - She got an "F" in sex.

♦ ♦ ♦

190. What did Kamala name her pet zebra? - Spot.

♦ ♦ ♦

191. Why doesn't Kamala swim in the ocean? - Because they can't get the smell out of the Tuna.

♦ ♦ ♦

192. What do you call four liberals in a Volkswagen? – Far-from-thinkin

♦ ♦ ♦

193. Why doesn't Kamala eat Jell-O? - She can't figure out how to get two cups of hot water into those little packages.

♦ ♦ ♦

194. Why does Kamala wear green lipstick? - Because red means stop.

♦ ♦ ♦

195. Why did Kamala fail her driver's test? – She wasn't use to the front seat.

196. What was Kamala's mating call when she was younger? – "I'm so drunk."

♦ ♦ ♦

197. What is Kamala's mating call now that she is much older? - Yelling "I said I'm drunk!!"

♦ ♦ ♦

198. Why does Kamala have TGIF printed on her shirts? – Tits Go In Front.

♦ ♦ ♦

199. What do you call Kamala between two Republicans? – A mental block.

♦ ♦ ♦

200. What can strike Kamala without even knowing it? – A thought.

♦ ♦ ♦

201. What does 'Bones" McCoy say before he performs brain surgery on Kamala? - "Space the final Frontier…."

♦ ♦ ♦

202. What is Kamala's favorite wine? -"Daaddy I want to be president"

♦ ♦ ♦

203. What do you call Kamala with a runny nose? – Full

♦ ♦ ♦

204. Why does Kamala take the pill? - So she knows what day of the week it is.

♦ ♦ ♦

205. What's the difference between Kamala and the Titanic? - They know how many men went down on the Titanic.

♦ ♦ ♦

206. What's the difference between Kamala and a pay phone? - It only cost 25 cents to use a pay phone.

♦ ♦ ♦

207. How do you keep a liberal in Suspense? (I'll tell you tomorrow.)

♦ ♦ ♦

208. What is the difference between liberal and a terrorist? - You can negotiate with a terrorist.

♦ ♦ ♦

209. What do you see when you look into Kamala's eyes? – The back of her head.

♦ ♦ ♦

210. What do you call Kamala at a college? - A Visitor.

♦ ♦ ♦

211. What do you call two nuns and Kamala? - Two tight ends and a wide receiver.

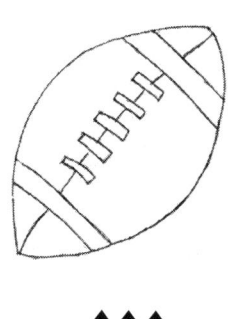

♦ ♦ ♦

212. .Did you know that Kamala once stayed up all night to see where the sun went? - It finally dawned on her.

♦ ♦ ♦

213. What does Kamala think an innuendo is? - An Italian suppository.

♦ ♦ ♦

214. What do you call a zit on Kamala's ass? - A brain tumor.

♦ ♦ ♦

215. What is the definition of gross ignorance? – 144 liberals.

♦ ♦ ♦

216. Kamala went to see her shrink the other day and he said "go ahead and lie down" and she said "why can't I lie standing up."

♦ ♦ ♦

217. What did Kamala do to become the Democrat nominee? - You know sometimes you just got to "Hawk Tuah" and spit on that thang.

♦ ♦ ♦

218. If Kamala is so smart, why do women get so mad when you tell them they are as smart as Kamala?

♦ ♦ ♦

219. Why does Kamala plug her ears? – She's trying to hold a thought.

♦ ♦ ♦

220. Kamala makes Blondes look smart again.

♦ ♦ ♦

221. What does Kamala think the last two words of the national anthem are? - Play ball!

♦ ♦ ♦

222. What did the Kamala's right leg say to the left leg? - Nothing, they haven't met!

♦ ♦ ♦

223. Why did Walz get a nipple ring? -Because Kamala got a Dick Cheney.

♦ ♦ ♦

224. Walz is a second story man, because no one believes his first story

♦ ♦ ♦

225. How did Trump get Kamala out of the coconut tree? - He just cut the damn thing down!

♦ ♦ ♦

226. Kamala is a real Coco-Nut case!

♦ ♦ ♦

227. Walz to Kamala "You're the Coco to my Nut!

♦ ♦ ♦

228. What joke is no longer funny? – Kamala Harris.

♦ ♦ ♦

229. I can not lie; I cut down the coconut tree. (Trump)

♦ ♦ ♦

230. While Kamala was doing "Call Her Daddy", Douglas was doing "Who's Your Nanny."

♦ ♦ ♦

231. Trump is the straw that broke the Kamala's back!

♦ ♦ ♦

232. There are some people that are liked wherever they go, and then there is Kamala.

♦ ♦ ♦

233. Kamala had a blood test in the morning, so she stayed up all night studying for it.

234. Who's your Daddy Kamala? – Donald Harris or Donald Trump? - I guess we'll find out after the election!

Mommy Mommy Jokes

1. Mommy! Mommy! My head hurts! Shut up kid and stop falling out of coconut trees!

◆ ◆ ◆ ◆

2. "Mommy, Mommy! I don't want to go to America!" "Shut up, and get back in the barrel!"

◆ ◆ ◆ ◆

3. "Mommy, Mommy! Is that Willy Brown's daughter?" "Shut up, what are you writing a book or something?"

◆ ◆ ◆ ◆

4. "Mommy, Mommy! Why is Kamala pushing the country off the cliff?" Shut up, before everyone wakes up!"

◆ ◆ ◆ ◆

5. "Mommy, Mommy! My hand hurts?" "Shut up, and keep filling out those ballots!"

◆ ◆ ◆ ◆

6. "Mommy, Mommy! Why does she keep Cackling?" "Shut up, and just keep picking up the damn eggs!"

Limericks

There once was a Harris so grime,
Whose open border plan was a crime.
She let them all come through,
With a welcome or two,
Now her policies are slime.

♦ ♦ ♦ ♦

There once was a Kamala I'm so fine,
Whose borders were open, oh what a crime!
She welcomed with cheer,
Untold millions each year,
Now her legacy's in quite in decline!

♦ ♦ ♦ ♦

There once was a creature so brine,
Aliens eating our pets in their prime.
They'd dine on a Pug,
With some Feline hug,
Now our houses are eerily swine.

♦ ♦ ♦ ♦

There once was a Kamala so bright,
Whose Vin diagram skills shone with great light.
She rode on a bus,
Yellow and full of fuss,
Where her charts and graphs sparkled with delight.

♦ ♦ ♦ ♦

There once was a Kamala so bright,
Whose Venn diagrams shone with great light.
She'd laugh with a grin,
Like a chicken within,
As she rode on a yellow bus in delight.

♦ ♦ ♦ ♦

There once was a Kamala so asinine,
Whose cackle was heard all the time.
She'd laugh with glee,
At Marxist decree,
Till her opponents felt quite genuine.

♦ ♦ ♦ ♦

There once was a Kamala so discline,

Whose laughter was heard all the time.
She'd cackle with glee,
As she plotted with thee,
In her Marxist vice presidential crimes.

♦ ♦ ♦ ♦

Kamala, the VP with a grin so wide,
Treasonous tales of her actions did reside.
Her cackle so shrill,
Marxist views stood still,
Incompetence her greatest pride.

♦ ♦ ♦ ♦

There once was Tampon Tim in the fray,
Chosen by Kamala, oh what to say?
He bled with each zeal,
Through his meetings so real,
Now his briefings are stained each day.

♦ ♦ ♦ ♦

There once was Kamala so borderline,
Whose border control was a crime.
She took all the dough,
And our guns in her go,
Now we're left with mere rhyme.

♦ ♦ ♦ ♦

Kamala, the border czar bright,
Lied about inflation with all her might.
She'd take all our guns,
And leave us with puns,
And a wallet that's slim and not right.

♦ ♦ ♦ ♦

There once was a Kalama so free,
Open borders brought chaos to see,
Inflation did stray,
Illegals came to stay,
Now prices are high as can see!

♦ ♦ ♦ ♦

There once was a Kamala so fine,
Whose lies shone with a certain design.
She'd spin with a grin,
As her tales came to spin,
And the truth was left far behind.

♦ ♦ ♦ ♦

There once was a Kamala so bright,
Whose identity was Biden in hindsight.
They switched with a grin,
In a dance to win,
Now both are confused, day and night!

♦ ♦ ♦ ♦

There once was a Harris so spite,
Jokes about her were told day and night.
She'd trip on her feet,
And her brain would retreat,
But her cackle was always so trite.

♦ ♦ ♦ ♦

There once was Kamala not so bright,
Claimed to make blonds clever over night.
She gave them a test,
With answers so blessed,
Now they're smart, and their hair is just right!

Quotes

"I can imagine what can be, and be unburdened by what has been."

♦ ♦ ♦ ♦

"So given where we are now, so no longer are you necessarily keeping those private files in some file cabinet that's locked in the basement of the house. It's on your laptop, and it's then therefore up here in this cloud that exists above us."

♦ ♦ ♦ ♦

"It is time for us to do what we have been doing. And that time is every day. Every day it is time for us to agree that there are things and tools that are available to us to slow this thing down."

♦ ♦ ♦ ♦

"We invested an additional $12 billion into community banks, because we know community banks are in the community, and understand the needs and desires of that community as well as the talent and capacity of community."

♦ ♦ ♦ ♦

"I love Venn diagrams. I really do, I love Venn diagrams. It's just something about those three circles"

"Who doesn't love a yellow school bus, right? Can you raise your hand if you love a yellow school bus? Many of us went to school on the yellow school bus, right?"

♦ ♦ ♦ ♦

"We also recognize just as it has been in the U.S. for Jamaica one of the issues that has been presented as an issue that is economic in the way its impact has been the pandemic. So to that end we are announcing today also that we will assist Jamaica in Covid recovery by assisting in terms of the recovery effort."

♦ ♦ ♦ ♦

"We have to stay woke. Like everybody needs to be woke. And you can talk about if you're the wokest or woker, but just stay more woke than less woke."

♦ ♦ ♦ ♦

"I think that to be very honest with you that I do believe that we should have rightly believed but we certainly believe that certain issues are just settled."

♦ ♦ ♦ ♦

"What else do we know about this population, 18 through 24? They are stupid! That is why we put them in dormitories. And they have a resident assistant. They make really bad decisions."

♦♦♦♦

"With us in government. We campaign with thee plan! Uppercase T uppercase P thee plan! And then the environment is such that we're expected to defend thee plan! (With a faux French accent)

♦♦♦♦

"Elections matter. And when folks vote, they order what they want — and in this case they got what they asked for."

♦♦♦♦

"So, Ukraine is a country in Europe. It exists next to another country called Russia. Russia is a bigger country. Russia is a powerful country. Russia decided to invade a smaller country called Ukraine. So, basically, that's wrong, and it goes against everything that we stand for."

♦♦♦♦

"But we all watched the television coverage of just yesterday. That's on top of everything else that we know and don't know yet, based on what we've just been able to see. And because we've seen it or not doesn't mean it hasn't happened."

♦ ♦ ♦ ♦

"Do not come. Do not come."

♦ ♦ ♦ ♦

"If somebody breaks into my house, they're getting shot," she said, laughing. "I probably should not have said that. My staff will deal with that later."

♦ ♦ ♦ ♦

"The United States shares a very important relationship, which is an alliance with the Republic of North Korea. And it is an alliance that is strong and enduring."

♦ ♦ ♦ ♦

"The significance of the passage of time, right? The significance of the passage of time. So when you think about it, there is great significance to the passage of time."

♦ ♦ ♦ ♦

"You know, when we talk about our children — I know for this group, we all believe that when we talk about the children of the community, they are a children of the community."

♦ ♦ ♦ ♦

"It seems like maybe it's a small issue; it's a big issue. You need to get to go and need to be able to get where you need to go to do the work and get home."

♦ ♦ ♦ ♦

"Well, I think that the concerns are based on what we should all be concerned about. But the solutions have to be and include what we are doing in terms of going forward, in terms of investments."

♦ ♦ ♦ ♦

"Fact-check: Biden is in good health, and I know of no reason why he should not be expected to live through a second term"

♦ ♦ ♦ ♦

"Bob and Doug returned to the Kennedy Space Center. They suited up. They waved to their families, and they rode an elevator up nearly 20 stories. They strapped in to their seats and waited as the tanks beneath filled with tens of thousands of gallons of fuel. And then they launched. Yeah, they did,"

♦ ♦ ♦ ♦

"And I haven't been to Europe"

♦ ♦ ♦ ♦

"Do you know that the women's teams were not allowed to have brackets until 2022?"

♦ ♦ ♦ ♦

"I have always believed, and I've worked on it, that the climate crisis is real, that it is an urgent matter to which we should apply metrics that include holding ourselves to deadlines around time."

♦ ♦ ♦ ♦

We have a secure border in that that is a priority for any nation, including ours and our administration."

♦ ♦ ♦ ♦

"I will take him out tonight" (Maxine Waters)

♦ ♦ ♦ ♦

"Well, there are approximately 5 million, to your point Craig. We have to have a buyback program and I support a mandatory buyback program. It's got to be smart, we got to do it the right way, but there are 5 million at least some estimate as many as 10 million and we're going to have to have smart public policy that's about taking those off the streets."

♦ ♦ ♦ ♦

"I grew up in a middle class family "

♦ ♦ ♦ ♦

"I support buybacks." The forum moderator then asked Harris, "How mandatory is your gun buyback program?" Harris made clear, "It's mandatory."

♦ ♦ ♦ ♦

"I worked fries"

♦ ♦ ♦ ♦

"There was a little girl in California, who was part of the second class to integrate her public schools, and she was bused to school every day, and that little girl was me."

♦ ♦ ♦ ♦

"It is status-quo thinking to believe that putting more police on the streets creates more safety. That's wrong. It's just wrong."

♦ ♦ ♦ ♦

"We did it Joe"

♦ ♦ ♦ ♦

"The bread cost more, the gas costs more and we have to understand what that means. That's about the cost of living going up."

♦ ♦ ♦ ♦

"Just because you legally possess a gun in the sanctity of your locked home doesn't mean that we're not going to walk into that home and check to see if you're being responsible."

♦ ♦ ♦ ♦

"If somebody breaks into my house, they're getting shot"

♦ ♦ ♦ ♦

"We will work together, and continue to work together, to address these issues…and to work together as we continue to work, operating from the new norms, rules, and agreements, that we will convene to work together…we will work on this together."

♦ ♦ ♦ ♦

"We got to take this stuff seriously, as seriously as you are because you have been forced to have taken this seriously."

♦ ♦ ♦ ♦

"It is time for us to do what we have been doing. And that time is every day."

♦ ♦ ♦ ♦

"And I Met with President Zelensky, I shared with him American intelligence"

♦ ♦ ♦ ♦

"Yes, I just did do DEI."

♦ ♦ ♦ ♦

"AI is a kind of a fancy thing. It's first of all 2 letters. It means artificial intelligence."

♦ ♦ ♦ ♦

Today is today, and yesterday is today yesterday. Tomorrow will be today tomorrow, so live today so the future will be as the past today as it is tomorrow."

♦ ♦ ♦ ♦

"The first battle ground is to rewrite history" "to be unburdened by what was", basically to lie about the past. Karl Marx the father of Socialism

♦ ♦ ♦ ♦

"A loaf of bread cost 50% more today than it before the pandemic. Ground beef is up almost 50%."

♦ ♦ ♦ ♦

"The wheels on the bus go round and round."

♦ ♦ ♦ ♦

"That we are each endowed with the right to liberty and the pursuit of happiness"

◆ ◆ ◆ ◆

"Well, if you are hardworking, if you have the dreams and the ambitions and the aspirations of what I believe you do, you're in my plan." You know, I have to tell you, I really love and am so energized by what I know to be the spirit and character of the American people. We have ambition. We have aspirations. We have dreams. We can see what's possible. We have an incredible work ethic, but not everyone has the access to the opportunities that allow them to achieve these things. But we don't lack for those things."

◆ ◆ ◆ ◆

"Mr. Vice President, I'm speaking, I'm speaking."

◆ ◆ ◆ ◆

"Do I see people testifyin'… Can I get a witness?" (In a fake cringe accent)

♦ ♦ ♦ ♦

"On this issue for example we applaud Germany in terms of what it has done as it relates to Nordstream 2, as it relates to what we need to do domestically as well as what we need to do in terms of this issue generally we have as the president said reevaluated what we're doing in terms of the strategic oil reserves here in the United States to make sure that it will not have an impact or we can mitigate the impact on the American consumer."

♦ ♦ ♦ ♦

"The importance of community banks is they are, as they are called, they're in the community."

♦ ♦ ♦ ♦

[On sexual assault accusers against Joe Biden] "I believe them and I respect them being able to tell their story and having the courage to do it."

♦ ♦ ♦ ♦

"You need to get to go, and you to be able to get where you need to go, to do the work, and get home."

♦ ♦ ♦ ♦

What else do we know about this population, 18 through 24? They are stupid. That is why we put them in dormitories. And they have a resident assistant. They make really bad decisions.

♦ ♦ ♦ ♦

[On abortion] "So I think it's very important, as you have heard from so many incredible leaders for us at every moment in time and certainly this one, to see the moment in time in which we exist and are present, and to be able to contextualize it, to understand where we exist in the history and in the moment as it relates not only to the past but the future."

♦ ♦ ♦ ♦

"When we invest in clean energy and electric vehicles and reduce population, more of our children can breathe clean air and drink clean water."

♦ ♦ ♦ ♦

"I learned, I think I was I don't know 22 when I started that work, I learned that with the swipe of my pen I could charge someone with the lowest level offence and because of the swipe of my pen that person could be arrested they could sit in jail for at least 48 hours. They could lose time from work and their family maybe lose their job they'd have to come out of their own pocket to help hire a lawyer, they'd lose standing in their community all because of the swipe of my pen. Weeks later I could dismiss the charges but their life would forever be changed. So I learned at a very young age the power."

♦ ♦ ♦ ♦

"I said I'm going to the border and I" ("When are you going to the border, Vice President?") "I'm not finished!"

♦ ♦ ♦ ♦

"Half my families from Jamaica, are you kidding me?' (On legalization of marijuana)

♦ ♦ ♦ ♦

Kamala's DAD, Donald Harris "My dear departed grandmothers, as well as deceased parents must be turning in their graves right now." "Speaking for myself and my immediate Jamaican family, we wish to categorically dissociate ourselves from this travesty."

♦ ♦ ♦ ♦

Excuse me, are you his daughter?" an unidentified woman asks Harris, who is standing next to a distracted Brown, in the clip from a 1995 "PrimeTime Live" video package After a second of stunned silence, Harris responded, "No, I'm not."

♦ ♦ ♦ ♦

Walz: "I plan on waking up with Kamala."

Recipes

__Harris Slutty Salsa__

Ingredients

- 2 (14.5-ounce) cans diced fire-roasted tomatoes, one can drained & one can with juices
- ¼ small onion
- 3 large cloves garlic
- 1 jalapeño
- 1 bunch fresh cilantro
- Juice from a lime
- 1 teaspoon of honey
- 1 teaspoon salt
- Freshly ground black pepper, to taste
- ½ teaspoon ground cumin
- ¼ teaspoon Chile pepper powder

Combine all ingredients in a bowl and mix with a fork. Refrigerate for one hour before serving. Serve with your favorite chip.

Walz Creamy Horseradish Sause

Ingredients

- 2 Tablespoons grated horseradish
- 1/2 cup sour cream
- 3 Tablespoons mayonnaise
- 3 Tablespoons heavy cream
- 1 Tablespoon Dijon mustard
- 1 Tablespoon apple cider vinegar
- 1/2 teaspoon Kosher salt
- 1/2 teaspoon black pepper
- 1/4 teaspoon cayenne pepper

♦♦♦♦

Heals-Up-Hot Doggie

Ingredients

- 1 all-beef hot dog
- 1 hot dog bun
- 1 tablespoon yellow mustard
- 1 tablespoon sweet pickle relish
- 1 tablespoon chopped onion
- 2 tomato wedges
- 1 dill pickle spear
- 2 sport peppers
- 1 dash celery salt

OPEN BORDER TACOS

Ingredients

- 1 tablespoon vegetable oil
- 1 lb. ground beef
- 1 teaspoon ground cumin
- 1 teaspoon chili powder
- 1/2 teaspoon garlic powder
- 1/2 teaspoon dried oregano
- 1/2 teaspoon salt
- 1/4 teaspoon ground black pepper
- 2 tablespoons tomato paste
- 1/4 cup water
- 8 flour tortillas
- 1 cup Mexican cheese blend, shredded
- 2 medium tomatoes, diced
- 1 medium white onion, diced
- 1/4 cup fresh cilantro, finely chopped
- 1/4 cup sour cream (optional)
- 1 lime, wedged
- Heat oil in a large pan for 2 minutes over medium-high heat until the hot oil sizzles. Add ground beef and stir well to cook evenly until browned, about 6-8 minutes. Make sure

to break up beef into small pieces to help even browning.

- Add cumin, chili powder, paprika, garlic powder, oregano, salt, pepper, tomato paste and water. Reduce heat to medium and let the mixture simmer for 3-5 minutes until the sauce thickens a bit, stirring occasionally. Turn off heat and set aside.

- Heat the soft flour tortillas according to the package instructions, or heat in an ungreased skillet over medium-high heat for 30 seconds per side. You can also heat it directly on a gas burner for a few seconds to get char marks on the edges.

- Add 2-3 tablespoons of the ground beef mixture on each tortilla. Top with cheese, onion, tomato and cilantro. Add a dollop of sour cream and a squeeze of fresh lime juice, to taste.

Word Salad

Ingredients

- 2 small heads of soft lettuce, butter lettuce or similar
- 2 table spoons Lemon Vinaigrette
- 1 cucumber, thinly sliced
- ¼ cup shaved Parmesan cheese
- 2 tablespoons pumpkin seeds
- 1 avocado, thinly sliced
- ¼ cup microgreens

Roasted Tamari Almonds

- ½ cup raw almonds
- ½ tablespoon soy sauce

Instructions

1. Roast the almonds: Preheat the oven to 350°F and line a baking sheet with parchment paper. Place the almonds on the sheet and toss with tamari. Bake for 10 to 14 minutes or until browned. Remove from the oven and let cool for 5 minutes.

2. Assemble the salad. In a large bowl toss the lettuce with a few spoonful of the lemon vinaigrette. Add the cucumber,

parmesan, pumpkin seeds, avocado, and almonds. Drizzle with more dressing and top with microgreens.

Slick Willy Brown Rice and Chicken

Ingredients

- 1 tsp salt
- 1 tsp ground pepper
- 1 tsp onion powder
- 1 tsp garlic powder
- 1.5 lbs. boneless skinless chicken breasts
- 3 tbsp. olive oil divided
- ½ white onion chopped
- 4 garlic cloves minced
- 1 cup chicken broth
- 12 ounce frozen steam in bag broccoli cooked
- 3 cups cooked brown rice
- ⅓ Cup grated parmesan cheese you can also use grated Romano cheese.
- 1 ½ cups shredded sharp cheddar cheese

Instructions

1. In a small bowl mix together the salt, pepper, onion powder, and garlic powder.
2. Place the chicken onto a cutting board and cut into chunks or strips. Sprinkle the

seasoning on the chicken. Set the chicken aside.

3. Heat a couple of tablespoons of olive oil over medium-high heat, and once it's hot, add the chicken. Cook until browned on both sides, cooked through, and no longer pink on the inside. Remove the chicken from the pan and set it aside.

4. Heat another tablespoon of olive oil, add the onions, and cook for about 3-4 minutes or until translucent.

5. Add in the garlic and cook for another 2 minutes until fragrant.

6. Then pour in the chicken broth and bring it to a boil. Reduce to a simmer and let it cook down for about 2-3 minutes.

7. Then, stir in the broccoli, rice, and add the chicken back into the pot. Please note you should cook the frozen "steam in bag" broccoli ahead of time using the microwave instructions on the back of the bag.

8. Give the chicken and rice mixture a couple of stirs and let it cook for about 2-3 minutes until the broccoli and chicken are hot. There should still be some chicken broth at the bottom of the pan. Don't worry; the rice will absorb this and create a creamy, cheesy sauce in the next step.

Marxist Porridge

Ingredients

- 1 cup whole oat groats, soaked overnight* (SEE NOTE)
- 4 cups additional water
- Pinch of salt

Instructions

Drain and rinse the oat groats and transfer them to a blender. Add 4 cups fresh water salt and pulse until the grains are coarsely ground. Pour into a medium pot and bring to a boil over high heat, whisking frequently. Cover the pot, reduce the heat to low, and simmer for 30 minutes, stirring occasionally to prevent sticking, until the grains are soft and the porridge is creamy. Serve hot, with desired toppings.

Notes

*You CANNOT substitute rolled oats or steel cut oats for the oat groats in this recipe because the water ratio will be incorrect and your porridge will not thicken.

Crazy Kamala Cat Skewers

- Marinade:
- 2 pounds "Cat"
- 2 tsp black pepper
- 2 tsp ground cumin
- 2 tsp ground coriander
- 1 tsp turmeric
- 2 tsp chopped garlic
- 2 tbsp. sugar
- 2 tbsp. vegetable oil
- 2 tbsp. soya sauce
- 2 tbsp. lemon juice
- 2 tsp fish sauce
- Bamboo skewers

Method:

Cut the "Cat" into 1/4 inch slices or some sort of manageable pieces to weave onto a stick. Small skewers are best, but for some reason I can never find these and have to use long ones which are not as cute. Try to find small ones for cuteness sake.

Mix all of the ingredients together with a whisk in a bowl and then add the "Cat" slices. Let the "cat" marinate for 2 to 24 hours (in the fridge, obviously). Put the "cat' on the skewers and grill until cooked. (Soak the skewers for a little while before the skewering begins)

Spicy Peanut Sauce:

6 oz. roasted unsalted peanuts

2 cans of coconut milk

1/2 can (or 2-3 tbsps.) of red curry paste (I like the Maseri brand in the little red can)

2 tbsp. sugar

3 tbsp. lemon juice

1.5 tbsp. fish sauce

Directions

Process the peanuts in a food processor until they are a fine meal.

Empty one can of coconut milk in a pot and bring to a boil

Add red curry paste and mix together

Bring to a boil for 10-12 minutes until the oil from the coconut milk starts to rise to the top

Add the other can of coconut milk and the other ingredients and mix. Lower the heat to medium-low and allow to boil (gently and stirring often) for 15-20 minutes until the sauce has thickened and the oil has returned to the top.

Turn off heat and allow to rest for a half hour. Use peanut sauce indiscriminately.

Walz Glizzy Soup

Ingredients

- 100 g of boiled dog meat
- 500 g of gravy
- 20 g of green onion
- 10 g of a leek
- 10 g of perilla leaves
- 100 g of taro stalk soaked in water
- 8 g of salt
- 2 g of mashed garlic
- 3 g of perilla
- 2 g of red pepper
- 2 g of mashed ginger
- a little amount of pepper

Directions

1. After boiling the meat with gravy and stalk of taro for some time, boil again after putting vegetables and other ingredients into it.

2. Before eating, sprinkle pepper on it and put into an earthen bowl.

3. The stalk of taro is to be kept in cold water one or two days to get rid of its smell and taste.

Jamaican me crazy gumbo

Ingredients

- 2 pounds chicken thigh, skinless
- salt and pepper,
- ¼ cup canola oil
- 8 ounces smoked sausage
- ¼ cup unsalted butter
- ½ cup flour
- 1 medium onion, diced
- 2 teaspoons minced garlic
- 1 medium green bell pepper, diced
- 1 cup chopped celery
- ½ pound crab legs
- 1 tablespoon Creole Seasoning
- 1 tablespoon chicken bouillon powder
- ½ tablespoon smoked paprika
- 1 tablespoon thyme, fresh or dried
- 2 bay leaves
- 1 14- ounce can tomatoes, chopped
- 6 cups chicken stock or substitute with water
- 1 pound shrimp, peeled and deveined
- 1 tablespoon gumbo file
- 2 green onions , chopped
- ¼ cup parsley. Chopped

Instructions

- Lightly season the chicken with salt and pepper.
- Heat the oil over medium heat in a heavy-bottomed Dutch oven. Then cook the chicken until browned on both sides, remove, and set aside. Add the sausage and brown, and then remove. Set aside.
- Melt the butter and oil in a large Dutch oven or heavy-bottomed saucepan, then add the flour and stir until smooth.
- Cook on medium heat, stirring continuously, for about 20-30 minutes or until it turns a rich dark brown color – just like chocolate. Don't walk away from the stove during this process, or it could burn.
- When you have achieved your desired color, remove the Dutch oven from the stove and let it cool.
- Return the Dutch oven to the stove. Add the onion, garlic, green pepper, and celery, and cook for 8-10 minutes–stirring frequently.
- Then add chicken, sausage, crab legs, Creole seasoning, chicken bouillon or cubes, paprika, thyme, bay leaves, and let it cook for 5 minutes.
- Follow with the canned tomatoes and about 6 cups of chicken stock, then bring it all to a boil and simmer it for 45-50 minutes. After that, add the shrimp and simmer for 5 more minutes.
- Stir in file powder, green onions, and parsley. Adjust the soup's thickness and flavor with broth or water and salt.

Greens New Deal

Greens Wash Solution

- 1/2 cup white distilled vinegar
- 3 tablespoons salt

Ingredients

- 2 bunches fresh collard greens
- 1 tablespoon extra-virgin olive oil
- ½ cup finely diced onions
- 1 tablespoon minced garlic
- ½ teaspoon red pepper flakes
- 4-5 cups chicken broth
- 1 fully-cooked smoked turkey leg or wing
- 1 tablespoon white distilled vinegar
- Applewood smoked salt & black pepper, to season

Directions

Prep the Collard Greens

- Prepare the collard greens bath by filling your kitchen sink with cool water and adding vinegar and salt.
- Remove the collard greens from the steams by folding them in half lengthwise

and pulling the leaf away from the stem. (discard the stem)

- Place the collard greens into the prepared water bath and swish them around several times, scrubbing them to help loosen up any dirt.

- Let the collard greens soak for 15-20 minutes, giving them a scrub midway. Drain the water and refill with plain water and allow the greens to soak again if needed. Repeat as many times as needed until the water is free from any dirt or grit. After the final soak, drain the water. Next, rinse and scrub each leaf front and back with cool water to ensure they are clean.

- Tear the greens into bite-sized pieces and set them aside.

Cook the Greens

- In a large pot, heat olive oil. Add onions and sauté until tender.

- Add garlic and red pepper flakes and cook until garlic is fragrant.

- Pour in the broth and add the turkey leg. Bring to a boil.

- Add collard greens and reduce heat to a simmer.

- Cover and cook collard for 1 hour (or longer depending on your desired tenderness), stirring regularly.

- Once done, stir and then taste the broth and the greens. (add a little water if the broth is too bold for your liking)
- Stir in vinegar and smoked salt, and black pepper if desired.

Deserts

Crazy Cackling Coconut Cream Pie

Ingredients

- 1 9-inch pre-baked pie crust *
- 1 cup shredded sweetened coconut, divided
- 4 large egg yolks
- 1/3 cup cornstarch divided
- 14 ounce canned unsweetened coconut milk
- 1 1/4 cups whole milk, divided
- 1/2 cup + 2 Tablespoons granulated sugar
- 1/4 teaspoon salt
- 3 Tablespoons unsalted butter, room temperature*
- 1 teaspoon vanilla extract, diced
- 1/2 teaspoon coconut extract, to taste

For Topping:

- 1 1/2 cup heavy cream, lightly sweetened
- 3-4 Tablespoons powdered sugar, to

sweeten
- 1/2 teaspoon vanilla extract

Instructions

1. Toast coconut Add coconut to a large skillet. Cook over medium-low heat, stirring and tossing frequently, until the flakes are mostly golden brown. Remove from heat and transfer to a bowl to cool completely. Set aside, to cool.
2. Mix egg yolks, cornstarch and ¼ cup of milk in a bowl. Set aside
3. In medium saucepan combine remaining 1 cup milk, can of coconut milk, granulated sugar and the salt. Set mixture over medium heat, and bring to a simmer, stirring occasionally.
4. Temper eggs: Spoon a ladleful of simmering milk and, while mixing with a fork, pour a slow steady stream into the bowl with the beaten eggs, mixing well, to temper the eggs (warm them up slowly). Repeat with another spoonful of simmering milk.
5. Combine: Pour the egg yolk mixture into saucepan, stirring constantly. Cook, stirring vigorously, for 2-3 minutes, until thickened.
6. Remove from heat and stir butter, vanilla extract and coconut extract, stirring until butter has melted. Stir in 3/4 cup of the toasted coconut (reserve the rest for topping on the finished pie).
7. Cool: Pour warm filling into cooled, baked pie crust. Lay a piece of plastic wrap directly over the surface of the pudding and refrigerate for at least 4 hours or overnight.
8. Whipped cream: Add cream, powdered sugar and vanilla to a bowl and beat with electric mixers

until peaks form. Pipe or smooth whipped cream over pie filling. Top with remaining toasted coconut.

Banks Vanilla Milkshake

Ingredients

- 2 cups vanilla ice cream
- 1 cup whole milk
- 1 teaspoon vanilla extract

Directions

1. Gather all ingredients.
2. Blend ice cream, milk, and vanilla extract together in a blender until smooth.
3. Pour into glasses and serve.

Walz-nut Cake

Ingredients

- 2/3 cup Butter softened
- 1 cup Brown sugar
- 1 cup Granulated sugar
- 2 teaspoon Vanilla extract
- ½ teaspoon Kosher salt
- 2 teaspoon Cinnamon
- ½ teaspoon Nutmeg
- 5 Eggs
- ⅓ cup Vegetable oil
- ½ cup Sour cream full fat
- 1 cup Buttermilk
- 3 cups Cake flour
- 3 teaspoon Baking powder
- 2 cups Walnuts

Instructions

- Preheat an oven to 180c (350f). Butter the Bundt cake pan with room temperature butter and flour to prevent the cake from sticking to the pan.
- Into a large mixing bowl, add the softened

butter, brown sugar, granulated sugar, cinnamon, nutmeg, kosher salt, and vanilla extract and mix with an electric hand mixer until it's creamy.

- Add the room temperature eggs, oil, and mix until combined.

- Add the full fat sour cream and mix well until well combined.

- Add ½ of the flour and the baking powder, and ½ of the buttermilk, and mix until almost combined.

- Add the rest of the flour and the buttermilk and mix until almost combined. Add the chopped and toasted walnuts and mix until just combined and there are no lumps of flour visible. Don't overmix!

- Pour the batter to the prepared cake pan and bake in a 180c (350f) oven for 50-60 minutes or until a toothpick inserted into the cake comes out clean.

- Allow the cake to cool to room temperature before flipping the cake. Top the pan with a plate, flip the cake and tap the cake pan to release the cake from the pan.

- Sprinkle the cake with powdered sugar or caramel sauce.

Canadian Depression Cake

(Grandpere dans le Sirop)

Ingredients

- 2 cups packed brown sugar
- 2 cups water
- 1 tablespoon butter
- ½ teaspoon vanilla extract
- 2 cups all-purpose flour
- 1 cup white sugar
- 1 tablespoon baking powder
- 1 pinch salt
- ⅓ cup cold butter
- ¾ cup milk
- 1 teaspoon vanilla extract

Directions

1. In a large saucepan, mix together the brown sugar and water, and bring to a boil. Reduce heat to low, and stir in 1 tablespoon of butter and 1/2 teaspoon of vanilla. Cover while preparing the batter.

2. In a medium bowl, stir together the flour, white sugar, baking powder and salt. Cut in 1/3 cup of butter by pinching between your fingers, or using a fork until the

mixture has lumps no larger than crumbs. Make a well in the center, and pour in the milk and 1 teaspoon of vanilla all at once. Stir just until all of the dry mixture is absorbed.

3. Return the sugar mixture to a full boil, and drop large spoonful's of the batter into the syrup. Cover and simmer over medium heat, without removing the lid, for 15 minutes, or until a toothpick inserted into the largest dumpling comes out clean.

Cocktails

__Fake White Russian dossier__

Ingredients:

- 1.5 oz. Baileys Espresso Crème Liqueur
- 0.5 oz. Smirnoff Vodka
- 0.25 oz. Coffee liqueur
- 2 oz. Milk
- Maraschino Cherry
- Ice

Directions:

Pour all ingredients into a glass with ice and stir Combine in a glass and mix...

◆ ◆ ◆ ◆

__Tampon Tim__

Ingredients:

1 1/2 oz. Scotch Whisky, 5/6 oz. Sweet Vermouth, Dash Angostura Bitters

Preparation:

Add ingredients to a mixing glass and stir over ice, strain into a chilled glass, garnish and serve straight up, or mix in rocks glass, filled with ice.

♦ ♦ ♦ ♦

Tampon Timmy

Ingredients:

Glass of cola drink, Splash of grenadine syrup

Directions:

Add a splash of grenadine to a glass of cola, garnish with a maraschino cherry.

♦ ♦ ♦ ♦

Open Borders Margarita

Ingredients:

- 1 pinch kosher salt for rimming glasses
- ice cubes
- ½ cup silver tequila
- ¼ cup sweetened lime juice

- ¼ cup triple sec
- ¼ cup lemon-lime soda

Directions:

1. Rim 2 margarita glasses with salt, if desired, and fill with ice. Pour tequila, sweetened lime juice, triple sec, and lemon-lime soda into a shaker filled with ice, hold your hand firmly over the top of the shaker so it doesn't pop off from the carbonated soda. Shake vigorously. Pour into prepared margarita glasses, and serve.

♦ ♦ ♦ ♦

Terrorist - Tini

Ingredients:

- 1 1/2 oz. Vodka
- 1 oz. lemon juice
- 3/4 oz. simple syrup
- 1/2 oz. pomegranate juice
- 1 maraschino cherry

Directions:

- Add Vodka, lemon juice, and simple syrup to a shaker with ice.
- Shake and strain into a chilled martini glass.

- Sink pomegranate juice by pouring slowly over the back of a spoon into cocktail.
- Drop in one maraschino cherry

♦ ♦ ♦ ♦

Civil Disobedience Cocktail

1 1/2 oz. of Jamaican rum

3/4 oz. of sweet vermouth

3/4 oz. of JAGERMEISTER LIQUEUR

Kamala Medical Terms

Acute: Opposite of an ugly.

Anally -- occurring yearly

Artery -- study of paintings

Bacteria -- back door of cafeteria

Barium -- what doctors do when treatment fails

Benign: What you are after you be eight.

Blood: A type of Gang.

Bowel -- letter like A.E.I.O.U

Caesarian section -- district in Rome

Capsule: A space ship.

Cat scan -- searching for kitty

Cauterize -- Made eye contact with her

Clitoris: A type of flower.

Colic -- sheep dog

Coma -- a punctuation mark

Congenital – friendly

Concussion: A prisoner's sofa pillow.

Constipation: An important U.S. document.

D&C -- where Washington is

Diaphragm: A drawing in geometry.

Diarrhea -- journal of daily events

Dilate -- to live long

Dildo: Variety of sweet pickle.

Douche: Italian word for "12."

Enema -- not a friend

Erection: When the Japanese vote.

Femur: Not a Male.

Fester -- quicker

Fibula -- a small lie

Fracture: A number less than one.

Genes -- blue denim slacks

Genital -- non-Jewish

G.I. Series -- soldiers' ball game

Grippe -- suitcase

Hangnail – coathook

Heart: Bow & Arrow target.

High Colonic: Jewish religious holiday.

Hospital: An unknown person ejecting saliva.

Impotent -- distinguished, well known

Infection: Russians coming to the U.S.

Intense pain -- torture in a teepee

Jaundice: To include in a group.

Jaw: A shark without as much teeth.

Joint: A location or place.

Kinesthetics: A relationship towards relatives.

Labour pain -- got hurt at work

Laceration: Dainty material allotment.

Leper: A wild cat.

Lesbian: Person from the Middle East.

Lesion: A unit of Roman Army.

Loin: Not fat.

Lymph: A special Fairy.

Lymph Node: Where special Fairy lives.

Medical staff -- doctor's cane

Medicare: A partial care.

Meningitis: Getting a Man.

Menstrual cycle: Bloody vehicle for men.

Menstruation: Male Model display.

Midwife: Second wife in three marriages.

Migraine: Not your wheat.

Minor Operation: Coal digging

Miscarriage: Firing a Rifle and missing a target.

Morbid -- higher offer

Nitrate -- cheaper than day rate

Node -- was aware of

Organic: Musical.

Orgasm: Person who accompanies the church choir.

Outpatient -- person who had fainted

Ovaries: French egg dish made with cheese.

Pap smear -- fatherhood test

Pelvis -- cousin of Elvis

Post-operative -- letter carrier

Protein -- favouring young people

Rectum -- damn near killed 'em

Recovery room -- place to do upholstery

Rheumatic -- amorous

Scar -- rolled tobacco leaf

Secretion -- hiding anything

Seizure -- Roman emperor

Serology -- study of knighthood

Tablet -- small table

Testicles: Sucking sacks found on an octopus.

Terminal illness -- sickness at airport

Tibia -- country in North Africa

Tumour -- an extra pair

Ultrasound: A loud noise.

Umbilical Cord: Part of a parachute.

Urine -- opposite of you're out

Vagina: Heart trouble.

Varicose -- located nearby

Varicose Veins: Veins very close to each other.

Vein: Conceited.

Vein -- conceited

Weak: Seven days.

Zit: Dog Command.

The ultimate BLONDE joke book and other fun stuff

Coloring pages

Cat Lady

James Pace

Yellow Bus

The wheels on the bus go ...

Passage of time

Yellow School Bus

Word Salad

Venn Diagram

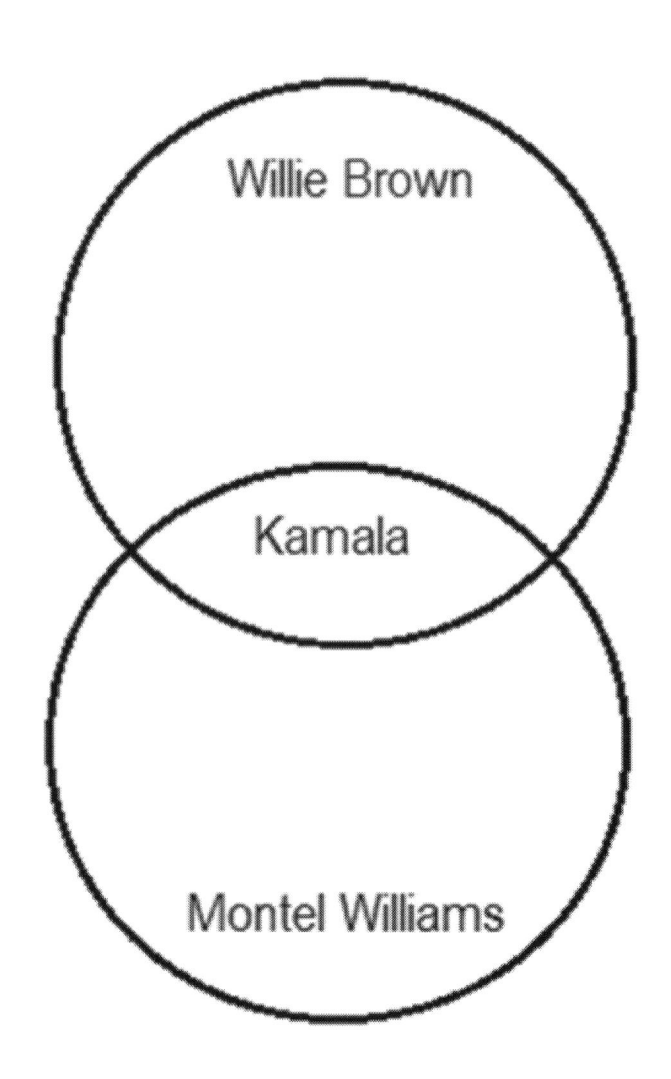

- Willie Brown
- Kamala
- Montel Williams

The ultimate BLONDE joke book and other fun stuff

The Cloud

James Pace

French Fries

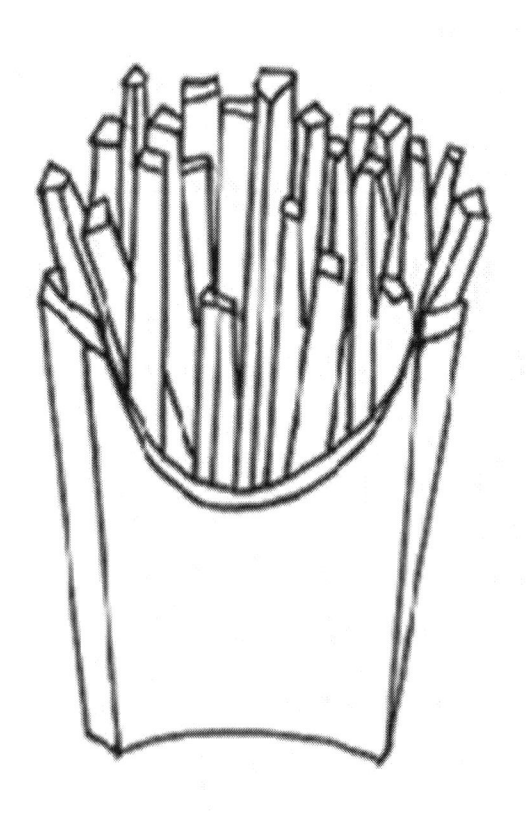

Coconut Tree

James Pace

Kamala's Border Wall

The ultimate BLONDE joke book and other fun stuff

More of Kamala's Border Wall

James Pace

WALZ

The ultimate BLONDE joke book and other fun stuff

Number Two

K A

M

A

L A 2

James Pace

Word Find

Crossword Puzzle

Down:
1. The China Virus.
2. Kamala's favorite Diagram.
3. Another word salad of Kamala's.
5. Kamala' leg up.
7. Where Kamala grew up.
9. Biden's VP
10. What Kamala's campaign run on.
11. Item that doubled in price during this administration.
14. 46th President.
17. Kamala's VP pick.
20. Something every country needs to be a country.

Across:
4. That thing between the US and Mexico that is wide open.
5. A very over used liberal term
6. Diversity, Equity, and Inclusion.
8. What Trump will do for this country.
12. Socialist principles and theories.
13. Kalama's one job.
15. Kamala claimed she was brought up in the
16. She was the last one in the room, 84 Billion lost.
18. Place where Kamala never worked.
19. Kamala's favorite ride.
21. 45th President.

Kalama

```
U J G E O R G E S O R O S A F
J G C T T I M E M T C B V H A
Z A A O A N Z R R P A O E E I
I S I A U C F S B S T R N A L
R W R H F U J O R L L D N D F
C A G Y I G B C O I A E D B A
O M I E L D H I W C D R I O I
C P N L L E Q A N K Y C A A L
O Q F L E B K L N W B Z G R E
N M L O G T A I T I V A R D D
U W A W A H M S R L S R A G B
T A T B L A A M U L W T M Y A
Z L I U S M L Z M I P Q A V R
V L O S O A A I P E M P T N O
D Y N G T S C U V X G K A M W
```

SlickWillie	Venn Diagram	Afghanistan	Wall
George Soros	Yellow Bus	Failed Bar	Fail
Headboard	Socialism	Catlady	CAIR
Illegals	Coconut	Inflation	Debt
Swamp	Time	Border Czar	FJB
Mr Brown	Kamala	Trump 2024	
Hamas			

James Pace

Crossword Puzzle

Down:
1. The China Virus.
2. Kamala's favorite Diagram.
3. Another word salad of Kamala's
5. Kamala" leg up.
7. Where Kamala grew up.
9. Biden's VP
10. What Kamala's campaign run on.
11. Item that doubled in price during this administration.
14. 46th President.
17. Kamala's VP pick.
20. Something every country needs to be a country.

Across:
4. That thing between the US and Mexico that is wide open.
5. A very over used liberal term
6. Diversity, Equity, and Inclusion.
8. What Trump will do for this country.
12. Socialist principles and theories
13. Kalama's one job.
15. Kamala claimed she was brought up in the
16. She was the last one in the room, 84 Billion lost.
18. Place where Kamala never worked.
19. Kamala's favorite ride.
21. 45th President.

Kalama

```
U J G E O R G E S O R O S A F
J G C T T I M E M T C B V H A
Z A A O A N Z R R P A O E E I
I S I A U C F S B S T R N A L
R W R H F U J O R L L D N D F
C A G Y I G B C O I A E D B A
O M I E L D H I W C D R I O I
C P N L L E Q A N K Y C A A L
O Q F L E B K L N W B Z G R E
N M L O G T A I T I V A R D D
U W A W A H M S R L S R A G B
T A T B L A A M U L W T M Y A
Z L I U S M L Z M I P Q A V R
V L O S O A A I P E M P T N O
D Y N G T S C U V X G K A M W
```

SlickWillie	Venn Diagram	Afghanistan	Wall
George Soros	Yellow Bus	Failed Bar	Fail
Headboard	Socialism	Catlady	CAIR
Illegals	Coconut	Inflation	Debt
Swamp	Time	Border Czar	FJB
Mr Brown	Kamala	Trump 2024	
Hamas			

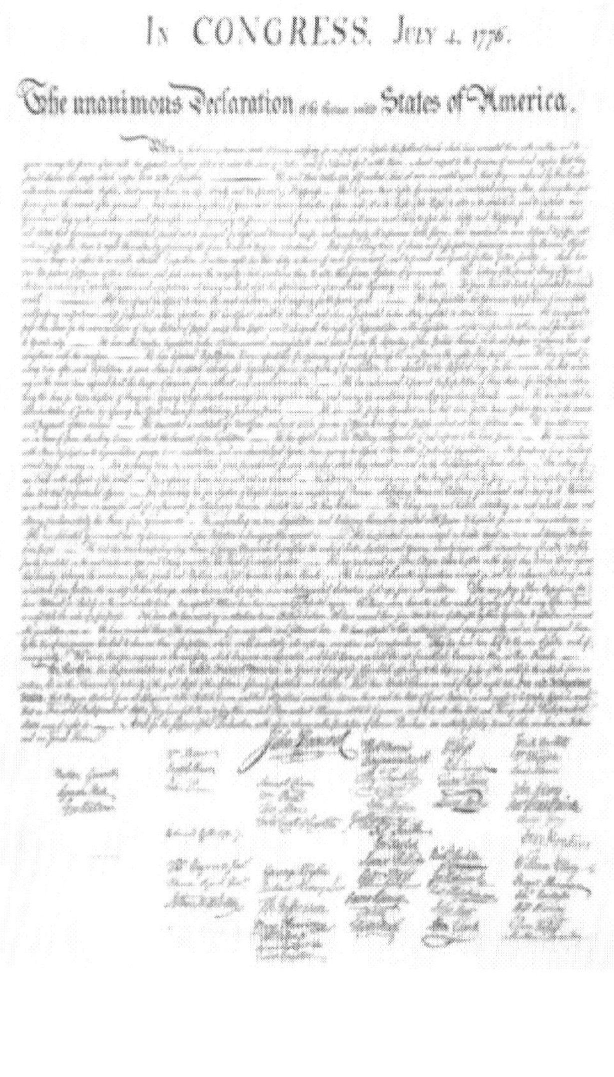

IN CONGRESS, JULY 4, 1776.

The unanimous Declaration of the thirteen united States of America.

The Declaration Of Independence

In Congress, July 4, 1776

The unanimous Declaration of the thirteen united States of America, When in the Course of human events, it becomes necessary for one people to dissolve the political bands which have connected them with another, and to assume among the powers of the earth, the separate and equal station to which the Laws of Nature and of Nature's God entitle them, a decent respect to the opinions of mankind requires that they should declare the causes which impel them to the separation.

We hold these truths to be self-evident, that all men are created equal, that they are endowed by their Creator with certain unalienable Rights, that among these are Life, Liberty and the pursuit of Happiness.-- That to secure these rights, Governments are instituted among Men, deriving their just powers from the consent of the governed, --That whenever any Form of Government becomes destructive of these ends, it is the Right of the People to alter or to abolish it, and to institute new Government, laying its foundation on such principles and organizing its powers in such form, as to them shall seem most likely to effect their Safety and Happiness. Prudence, indeed, will dictate that Governments long established should not be changed for light and transient causes; and accordingly all experience hath shewn, that mankind are more disposed to suffer, while evils are sufferable, than to right themselves by abolishing the forms to which they are accustomed. But when a long train of abuses and usurpations, pursuing invariably the same Object evinces a design to reduce them under absolute Despotism, it is their right, it is their duty, to throw off such Government, and to provide new Guards for their future security.--Such has been the patient sufferance of these Colonies; and such is now the necessity which constrains them to alter their former Systems of Government. The history of the present King of Great Britain is a history of repeated injuries and usurpations, all having in direct object the establishment of an absolute Tyranny over these States. To prove this, let Facts be submitted to a candid world.

He has refused his Assent to Laws, the most wholesome and necessary for the public good.

He has forbidden his Governors to pass Laws of immediate and pressing importance, unless suspended in their operation till his Assent should be obtained; and when so suspended, he has utterly neglected to attend to them.

He has refused to pass other Laws for the accommodation of large districts of people, unless those people would relinquish the right of Representation in the Legislature, a right inestimable to them and formidable to tyrants only.

He has called together legislative bodies at places unusual, uncomfortable, and distant from the depository of their public Records, for the sole purpose of fatiguing them into compliance with his measures.

He has dissolved Representative Houses repeatedly, for opposing with manly firmness his invasions on the rights of the people.

He has refused for a long time, after such dissolutions, to cause others to be elected; whereby the Legislative powers, incapable of Annihilation, have returned to the People at large for their exercise; the State remaining in the mean time exposed to all the dangers of invasion from without, and convulsions within.

He has endeavoured to prevent the population of these States; for that purpose obstructing the Laws for Naturalization of Foreigners; refusing to pass others to encourage their migrations hither, and raising the conditions of new Appropriations of Lands.

He has obstructed the Administration of Justice, by refusing his Assent to Laws for establishing Judiciary powers.

He has made Judges dependent on his Will alone, for the tenure of their offices, and the amount and payment of their salaries.

He has erected a multitude of New Offices, and sent hither swarms of Officers to harrass our people, and eat out their substance.

He has kept among us, in times of peace, Standing Armies without the Consent of our legislatures.

He has affected to render the Military independent of and superior to the Civil power.

He has combined with others to subject us to a jurisdiction foreign to our constitution, and unacknowledged by our laws; giving his Assent to their Acts of pretended Legislation:

For Quartering large bodies of armed troops among us:

For protecting them, by a mock Trial, from punishment for any Murders which they should commit on the Inhabitants of these States:

For cutting off our Trade with all parts of the world:

For imposing Taxes on us without our Consent:

For depriving us in many cases, of the benefits of Trial by Jury:

For transporting us beyond Seas to be tried for pretended offences:

For abolishing the free System of English Laws in a neighbouring Province, establishing therein an Arbitrary government, and enlarging its Boundaries so as to render it at once an example and fit instrument for introducing the same absolute rule into these Colonies:

For taking away our Charters, abolishing our most valuable Laws, and altering fundamentally the Forms of our Governments:

For suspending our own Legislatures, and declaring themselves invested with power to legislate for us in all cases whatsoever.

He has abdicated Government here, by declaring us out of his Protection and waging War against us.

He has plundered our seas, ravaged our Coasts, burnt our towns, and destroyed the lives of our people.

He is at this time transporting large Armies of foreign Mercenaries to compleat the works of death, desolation and tyranny, already begun with circumstances of Cruelty & perfidy scarcely paralleled in the most barbarous ages, and totally unworthy the Head of a civilized nation.

He has constrained our fellow Citizens taken Captive on the high Seas to bear Arms against their Country, to become the executioners of their friends and Brethren, or to fall themselves by their Hands.

He has excited domestic insurrections amongst us, and has endeavoured to bring on the inhabitants of our frontiers, the merciless Indian Savages, whose known rule of warfare, is an undistinguished destruction of all ages, sexes and conditions.

In every stage of these Oppressions We have Petitioned for Redress in the most humble terms: Our repeated Petitions have been answered only by repeated injury. A Prince whose character is thus marked by every act which may define a Tyrant, is unfit to be the ruler of a free people.

Nor have We been wanting in attentions to our Brittish brethren. We have warned them from time to time of attempts by their legislature to extend an unwarrantable jurisdiction over us. We have reminded them of the circumstances of our emigration and settlement here. We have appealed to their native justice and magnanimity, and we have conjured them by the ties of our common kindred to disavow these usurpations, which, would inevitably interrupt our connections and correspondence. They too have been deaf to the voice of justice and of consanguinity. We must, therefore, acquiesce in the necessity, which denounces our Separation, and hold them, as we hold the rest of mankind, Enemies in War, in Peace Friends.

We, therefore, the Representatives of the united

States of America, in General Congress, Assembled, appealing to the Supreme Judge of the world for the rectitude of our intentions, do, in the Name, and by Authority of the good People of these Colonies, solemnly publish and declare, That these United Colonies are, and of Right ought to be Free and Independent States; that they are Absolved from all Allegiance to the British Crown, and that all political connection between them and the State of Great Britain, is and ought to be totally dissolved; and that as Free and Independent States, they have full Power to levy War, conclude Peace, contract Alliances, establish Commerce, and to do all other Acts and Things which Independent States may of right do. And for the support of this Declaration, with a firm reliance on the protection of divine Providence, we mutually pledge to each other our Lives, our Fortunes and our sacred Honor

Georgia

Button Gwinnett

Lyman Hall

George Walton

North Carolina

William Hooper

Joseph Hewes

John Penn

South Carolina

Edward Rutledge

Thomas Heyward, Jr.

Thomas Lynch, Jr.

Arthur Middleton

Massachusetts

John Hancock

Maryland

Samuel Chase

William Paca

Thomas Stone

Charles Carroll of Carrollton

Virginia

George Wythe

Richard Henry Lee

Thomas Jefferson

Benjamin Harrison

Thomas Nelson, Jr.

Francis Lightfoot Lee

Carter Braxton

Pennsylvania

Robert Morris

Benjamin Rush

Benjamin Franklin

John Morton

George Clymer

James Smith

George Taylor

James Wilson

George Ross

Delaware

Caesar Rodney

George Read

Thomas McKean

New York

William Floyd

Philip Livingston

Francis Lewis

Lewis Morris

New Jersey

Richard Stockton

John Witherspoon

Francis Hopkinson

John Hart

Abraham Clark

New Hampshire

Josiah Bartlett

William Whipple

Massachusetts

Samuel Adams

John Adams

Robert Treat Paine

Elbridge Gerry

Rhode Island

Stephen Hopkins

William Ellery

Connecticut

Roger Sherman

Samuel Huntington

William Williams

Oliver Wolcott

New Hampshire

Matthew Thornto

THE
CONSTITUTION
of the United States

We the People *of the United States*

We the People of the United States, in Order to form a more perfect Union, establish Justice, insure domestic Tranquility, provide for the common defence, promote the general Welfare, and secure the Blessings of Liberty to ourselves and our Posterity, do ordain and establish this Constitution for the United States of America

Article. I.

SECTION. 1

All legislative Powers herein granted shall be vested in a Congress of the United States, which shall consist of a Senate and House of Representatives.

SECTION. 2

The House of Representatives shall be composed of Members chosen every second Year by the People of the several States, and the Electors in each State shall have the Qualifications requisite for Electors of the most numerous Branch of the State Legislature.

No Person shall be a Representative who shall not have attained to the Age of twenty five Years, and been seven Years a Citizen of the United States, and who shall not, when elected, be an Inhabitant of that State in which he shall be chosen.

[Representatives and direct Taxes shall be apportioned among the several States which may be included within this Union, according to their respective Numbers, which shall be determined by adding to the whole Number of free Persons, including those bound to Service for a Term of Years, and excluding Indians not taxed, three fifths of all other Persons.]* The actual Enumeration shall be made within three Years after the first Meeting of the Congress of the United States, and within every subsequent Term of ten Years, in such Manner as they shall by Law direct. The Number of Representatives shall not exceed one for every thirty Thousand, but each State shall have at Least one Representative; and until such enumeration shall be made, the State of New Hampshire shall be entitled to chuse three, Massachusetts eight, Rhode-Island and Providence Plantations one, Connecticut five, New-York six, New Jersey four, Pennsylvania eight, Delaware one, Maryland six, Virginia ten, North Carolina five, South Carolina five, and Georgia three.

When vacancies happen in the Representation from any State, the Executive Authority thereof shall issue Writs of Election to fill such Vacancies.

The House of Representatives shall chuse their Speaker and other Officers; and shall have the sole Power of Impeachment.

SECTION. 3

The Senate of the United States shall be composed of two Senators from each State, [chosen by the Legislature thereof,]* for six Years; and each Senator shall have one Vote.

Immediately after they shall be assembled in Consequence of the first Election, they shall be divided as equally as may be into three Classes. The Seats of the Senators of the first Class shall be vacated at the Expiration of the second Year, of the second Class at the Expiration of the fourth Year, and of the third Class at the Expiration of the sixth Year, so that one third may be chosen every second Year; [and if Vacancies happen by Resignation, or otherwise, during the Recess of the Legislature of any State, the Executive thereof may make temporary Appointments until the next Meeting of the Legislature, which shall then fill such Vacancies.]*

The ultimate BLONDE joke book and other fun stuff

No Person shall be a Senator who shall not have attained to the Age of thirty Years, and been nine Years a Citizen of the United States, and who shall not, when elected, be an Inhabitant of that State for which he shall be chosen.

The Vice President of the United States shall be President of the Senate, but shall have no Vote, unless they be equally divided.

The Senate shall chuse their other Officers, and also a President pro tempore, in the Absence of the Vice President, or when he shall exercise the Office of President of the United States.

The Senate shall have the sole Power to try all Impeachments. When sitting for that Purpose, they shall be on Oath or Affirmation. When the President of the United States is tried, the Chief Justice shall preside: And no Person shall be convicted without the Concurrence of two thirds of the Members present.

Judgment in Cases of Impeachment shall not extend further than to removal from Office, and disqualification to hold and enjoy any Office of honor, Trust or Profit under the United States: but the Party convicted shall nevertheless be liable and subject to Indictment, Trial, Judgment and Punishment, according to Law.

SECTION. 4

The Times, Places and Manner of holding Elections for Senators and Representatives, shall be prescribed in each State by the Legislature thereof; but the Congress may at any time by Law make or alter such Regulations, except as to the Places of chusing Senators.

The Congress shall assemble at least once in every Year, and such Meeting shall be [on the first Monday in December,] unless they shall by Law appoint a different Day.

SECTION. 5

Each House shall be the Judge of the Elections, Returns and Qualifications of its own Members, and a Majority of each shall constitute a Quorum to do Business; but a smaller Number may adjourn from day to day, and may be authorized to compel the Attendance of absent Members, in such Manner, and under such Penalties as each House may provide.

Each House may determine the Rules of its Proceedings, punish its Members for disorderly Behaviour, and, with the Concurrence of two thirds, expel a Member.

Each House shall keep a Journal of its Proceedings, and from time to time publish the same, excepting such Parts as may in their Judgment require Secrecy; and the Yeas and Nays of the Members of either House on any question shall, at the Desire of one fifth of those Present, be entered on the Journal.

Neither House, during the Session of Congress, shall, without the Consent of the other, adjourn for more than three days, nor to any other Place than that in which the two Houses shall be sitting.

SECTION. 6

The Senators and Representatives shall receive a Compensation for their Services, to be ascertained by Law, and paid out of the Treasury of the United States. They shall in all Cases, except Treason, Felony and Breach of the Peace, be privileged from Arrest during their Attendance at the Session of their respective Houses, and in going to and returning from the same; and for any Speech or Debate in either House, they shall not be questioned in any other Place.

No Senator or Representative shall, during the Time for which he was elected, be appointed to any civil Office under the Authority of the United States, which shall have been created, or the Emoluments whereof shall have been encreased during such time; and no Person holding any Office under the United States, shall be a Member of either House during his Continuance in Office.

CONSTITUTION OF THE UNITED STATES

SECTION. 7

All Bills for raising Revenue shall originate in the House of Representatives; but the Senate may propose or concur with Amendments as on other Bills.

Every Bill which shall have passed the House of Representatives and the Senate, shall, before it become a Law, be presented to the President of the United States; If he approve he shall sign it, but if not he shall return it, with his Objections to that House in which it shall have originated, who shall enter the Objections at large on their Journal, and proceed to reconsider it. If after such Reconsideration two thirds of that House shall agree to pass the Bill, it shall be sent, together with the Objections, to the other House, by which it shall likewise be reconsidered, and if approved by two thirds of that House, it shall become a Law. But in all such Cases the Votes of both Houses shall be determined by Yeas and Nays, and the Names of the Persons voting for and against the Bill shall be entered on the Journal of each House respectively. If any Bill shall not be returned by the President within ten Days (Sundays excepted) after it shall have been presented to him, the Same shall be a Law, in like Manner as if he had signed it, unless the Congress by their Adjournment prevent its Return, in which Case it shall not be a Law.

Every Order, Resolution, or Vote to which the Concurrence of the Senate and House of Representatives may be necessary (except on a question of Adjournment) shall be presented to the President of the United States; and before the Same shall take Effect, shall be approved by him, or being disapproved by him, shall be repassed by two thirds of the Senate and House of Representatives, according to the Rules and Limitations prescribed in the Case of a Bill.

SECTION. 8

The Congress shall have Power To lay and collect Taxes, Duties, Imposts and Excises, to pay the Debts and provide for the common Defence and general Welfare of the United States; but all Duties, Imposts and Excises shall be uniform throughout the United States;

To borrow Money on the credit of the United States;

To regulate Commerce with foreign Nations, and among the several States, and with the Indian Tribes;

To establish an uniform Rule of Naturalization, and uniform Laws on the subject of Bankruptcies throughout the United States;

To coin Money, regulate the Value thereof, and of foreign Coin, and fix the Standard of Weights and Measures;

To provide for the Punishment of counterfeiting the Securities and current Coin of the United States;

To establish Post Offices and post Roads;

To promote the Progress of Science and useful Arts, by securing for limited Times to Authors and Inventors the exclusive Right to their respective Writings and Discoveries;

To constitute Tribunals inferior to the supreme Court;

To define and punish Piracies and Felonies committed on the high Seas, and Offenses against the Law of Nations;

To declare War, grant Letters of Marque and Reprisal, and make Rules concerning Captures on Land and Water;

To raise and support Armies, but no Appropriation of Money to that Use shall be for a longer Term than two Years;

To provide and maintain a Navy;

To make Rules for the Government and Regulation of the land and naval Forces;

To provide for calling forth the Militia to execute the Laws of the Union, suppress Insurrections and repel Invasions;

To provide for organizing, arming, and disciplining, the Militia, and for governing such Part of them as may be employed in the Service of the United States, reserving to the States respectively, the Appointment of the Officers, and the Authority of training the Militia according to the discipline prescribed by Congress;

To exercise exclusive Legislation in all Cases whatsoever, over such District (not exceeding ten Miles square) as may, by Cession of particular States, and the Acceptance of Congress, become the Seat of the Government of the United States, and to exercise like Authority over all Places purchased by the Consent of the Legislature of the State in which the Same shall be, for the Erection of Forts, Magazines, Arsenals, dock-Yards and other needful Buildings; And

To make all Laws which shall be necessary and proper for carrying into Execution the foregoing Powers, and all other Powers vested by this Constitution in the Government of the United States, or in any Department or Officer thereof.

SECTION. 9

The Migration or Importation of such Persons as any of the States now existing shall think proper to admit, shall not be prohibited by the Congress prior to the Year one thousand eight hundred and eight, but a Tax or duty may be imposed on such Importation, not exceeding ten dollars for each Person.

The Privilege of the Writ of Habeas Corpus shall not be suspended, unless when in Cases of Rebellion or Invasion the public Safety may require it.

No Bill of Attainder or ex post facto Law shall be passed.

[No Capitation, or other direct, Tax shall be laid, unless in Proportion to the Census or Enumeration herein before directed to be taken.]*

No Tax or Duty shall be laid on Articles exported from any State.

No Preference shall be given by any Regulation of Commerce or Revenue to the Ports of one State over those of another, nor shall Vessels bound to, or from, one State, be obliged to enter, clear, or pay Duties in another.

No Money shall be drawn from the Treasury, but in Consequence of Appropriations made by Law; and a regular Statement and Account of the Receipts and Expenditures of all public Money shall be published from time to time.

No Title of Nobility shall be granted by the United States: And no Person holding any Office of Profit or Trust under them, shall, without the Consent of the Congress, accept of any present, Emolument, Office, or Title, of any kind whatever, from any King, Prince, or foreign State.

SECTION. 10

No State shall enter into any Treaty, Alliance, or Confederation; grant Letters of Marque and Reprisal; coin Money; emit Bills of Credit; make any Thing but gold and silver Coin a Tender in Payment of Debts; pass any Bill of Attainder, ex post facto Law, or Law impairing the Obligation of Contracts, or grant any Title of Nobility.

No State shall, without the Consent of the Congress, lay any Imposts or Duties on Imports or Exports, except what may be absolutely necessary for executing it's inspection Laws: and the net Produce of all Duties and Imposts, laid by any State on Imports or Exports, shall be for the Use of the Treasury of the United States; and all such Laws shall be subject to the Revision and Control of the Congress.

No State shall, without the Consent of Congress, lay any Duty of Tonnage, keep Troops, or Ships of War in time of Peace, enter into any Agreement or Compact with another State, or with a foreign Power, or engage in War, unless actually invaded, or in such imminent Danger as will not admit of delay.

Article. II.

SECTION. 1

The executive Power shall be vested in a President of the United States of America. He shall hold his Office during the Term of four Years, and, together with the Vice President, chosen for the same Term, be elected, as follows:

Each State shall appoint, in such Manner as the Legislature thereof may direct, a Number of Electors, equal to the whole Number of Senators and Representatives to which the State may be entitled in the Congress: but no Senator or Representative, or Person holding an Office of Trust or Profit under the United States, shall be appointed an Elector.

[The Electors shall meet in their respective States, and vote by Ballot for two Persons, of whom one at least shall not be an Inhabitant of the same State with themselves. And they shall make a List of all the Persons voted for, and of the Number of Votes for each; which List they shall sign and certify, and transmit sealed to the Seat of the Government of the United States, directed to the President of the Senate. The President of the Senate shall, in the Presence of the Senate and House of Representatives, open all the Certificates, and the Votes shall then be counted. The Person having the greatest Number of Votes shall be the President, if such Number be a Majority of the whole Number of Electors appointed; and if there be more than one who have such Majority, and have an equal Number of Votes, then the House of Representatives shall immediately chuse by Ballot one of them for President; and if no Person have a Majority, then from the five highest on the List the said House shall in like Manner chuse the President. But in chusing the President, the Votes shall be taken by States, the Representation from each State having one Vote; A quorum for this Purpose shall consist of a Member or Members from two thirds of the States, and a Majority of all the States shall be necessary to a Choice. In every Case, after the Choice of the President, the Person having the greatest Number of Votes of the Electors shall be the Vice President. But if there should remain two or more who have equal Votes, the Senate shall chuse from them by Ballot the Vice President.]*

The Congress may determine the Time of chusing the Electors, and the Day on which they shall give their Votes; which Day shall be the same throughout the United States.

No Person except a natural born Citizen, or a Citizen of the United States, at the time of the Adoption of this Constitution, shall be eligible to the Office of President; neither shall any person be eligible to that Office who shall not have attained to the Age of thirty five Years, and been fourteen Years a Resident within the United States.

In Case of the Removal of the President from Office, or of his Death, Resignation, or Inability to discharge the Powers and Duties of the said Office, the Same shall devolve on the Vice President, and the Congress may by Law provide for the Case of Removal, Death, Resignation or Inability, both of the President and Vice President, declaring what Officer shall then act as President, and such Officer shall act accordingly, until the Disability be removed, or a President shall be elected.]*

The President shall, at stated Times, receive for his Services, a Compensation, which shall neither be increased nor diminished during the Period for which he shall have been elected, and he shall not receive within that Period any other Emolment from the United States, or any of them.

Before he enter on the Execution of his Office, he shall take the following Oath or Affirmation:—"I do solemnly swear (or affirm) that I will faithfully execute the Office of President of the United States, and will to the best of my Ability, preserve, protect and defend the Constitution of the United States."

CONSTITUTION OF THE UNITED STATES

SECTION. 2

The President shall be Commander in Chief of the Army and Navy of the United States, and of the Militia of the several States, when called into the actual Service of the United States; he may require the Opinion, in writing, of the principal Officer in each of the executive Departments, upon any Subject relating to the Duties of their respective Offices, and he shall have Power to grant Reprieves and Pardons for Offenses against the United States, except in Cases of Impeachment.

He shall have Power, by and with the Advice and Consent of the Senate, to make Treaties, provided two thirds of the Senators present concur; and he shall nominate, and by and with the Advice and Consent of the Senate, shall appoint Ambassadors, other public Ministers and Consuls, Judges of the supreme Court, and all other Officers of the United States, whose Appointments are not herein otherwise provided for, and which shall be established by Law: but the Congress may by Law vest the Appointment of such inferior Officers, as they think proper, in the President alone, in the Courts of Law, or in the Heads of Departments.

The President shall have Power to fill up all Vacancies that may happen during the Recess of the Senate, by granting Commissions which shall expire at the End of their next Session.

SECTION. 3

He shall from time to time give to the Congress Information of the State of the Union, and recommend to their Consideration such Measures as he shall judge necessary and expedient; he may, on extraordinary Occasions, convene both Houses, or either of them, and in Case of Disagreement between them, with Respect to the Time of Adjournment, he may adjourn them to such Time as he shall think proper; he shall receive Ambassadors and other public Ministers; he shall take Care that the Laws be faithfully executed, and shall Commission all the Officers of the United States.

SECTION. 4

The President, Vice President and all civil Officers of the United States, shall be removed from Office on Impeachment for, and Conviction of, Treason, Bribery, or other high Crimes and Misdemeanors.

Article. III.

SECTION. 1

The judicial Power of the United States, shall be vested in one supreme Court, and in such inferior Courts as the Congress may from time to time ordain and establish. The Judges, both of the supreme and inferior Courts, shall hold their Offices during good Behaviour, and shall at stated Times, receive for their Services, a Compensation, which shall not be diminished during their Continuance in Office.

SECTION. 2

The judicial Power shall extend to all Cases, in Law and Equity, arising under this Constitution, the Laws of the United States, and Treaties made, or which shall be made, under their Authority;—to all Cases affecting Ambassadors, other public Ministers and Consuls;—to all Cases of admiralty and maritime Jurisdiction;—to Controversies to which the United States shall be a Party;—to Controversies between two or more States;—between a State and Citizens of another State;—[* between Citizens of different States, —between Citizens of the same State claiming Lands under Grants of different States, [and between a State, or the Citizens thereof, and foreign States, Citizens or Subjects.]*

In all Cases affecting Ambassadors, other public Ministers and Consuls, and those in which a State shall be Party, the supreme Court shall have original Jurisdiction. In all the other Cases before mentioned, the supreme Court shall have appellate Jurisdiction, both as to Law and Fact, with such Exceptions, and under such Regulations as the Congress shall make.

The Trial of all Crimes, except in Cases of Impeachment, shall be by Jury; and such Trial shall be held in the State where the said Crimes shall have been committed; but when not committed within any State, the Trial shall be at such Place or Places as the Congress may by Law have directed.

SECTION. 3

Treason against the United States, shall consist only in levying War against them, or in adhering to their Enemies, giving them Aid and Comfort. No Person shall be convicted of Treason unless on the Testimony of two Witnesses to the same overt Act, or on Confession in open Court.

The Congress shall have Power to declare the Punishment of Treason, but no Attainder of Treason shall work Corruption of Blood, or Forfeiture except during the Life of the Person attainted.

CONSTITUTION OF THE UNITED STATES

Article. IV.

SECTION. 1

Full Faith and Credit shall be given in each State to the public Acts, Records, and judicial Proceedings of every other State. And the Congress may by general Laws prescribe the Manner in which such Acts, Records and Proceedings shall be proved, and the Effect thereof.

SECTION. 2

The Citizens of each State shall be entitled to all Privileges and Immunities of Citizens in the several States.

A Person charged in any State with Treason, Felony, or other Crime, who shall flee from Justice, and be found in another State, shall on Demand of the executive Authority of the State from which he fled, be delivered up, to be removed to the State having Jurisdiction of the Crime.

No Person held to Service or Labour in one State, under the Laws thereof, escaping into another, shall, in Consequence of any Law or Regulation therein, be discharged from such Service or Labour, but shall be delivered up on Claim of the Party to whom such Service or Labour may be due?

SECTION. 3

New States may be admitted by the Congress into this Union; but no new State shall be formed or erected within the Jurisdiction of any other State; nor any State be formed by the Junction of two or more States, or Parts of States, without the Consent of the Legislatures of the States concerned as well as of the Congress.

The Congress shall have Power to dispose of and make all needful Rules and Regulations respecting the Territory or other Property belonging to the United States; and nothing in this Constitution shall be so construed as to Prejudice any Claims of the United States, or of any particular State.

SECTION. 4

The United States shall guarantee to every State in this Union a Republican Form of Government, and shall protect each of them against Invasion; and on Application of the Legislature, or of the Executive (when the Legislature cannot be convened) against domestic Violence.

Article. V.

The Congress, whenever two thirds of both Houses shall deem it necessary, shall propose Amendments to this Constitution, or, on the Application of the Legislatures of two thirds of the several States, shall call a Convention for proposing Amendments, which in either Case, shall be valid to all Intents and Purposes, as Part of this Constitution, when ratified by the Legislatures of three fourths of the several States, or by Conventions in three fourths thereof, as the one or the other Mode of Ratification may be proposed by the Congress; Provided that no Amendment which may be made prior to the Year One thousand eight hundred and eight shall in any Manner affect the first and fourth Clauses in the Ninth Section of the first Article; and that no State, without its Consent, shall be deprived of its equal Suffrage in the Senate.

Article. VI.

All Debts contracted and Engagements entered into, before the Adoption of this Constitution, shall be as valid against the United States under this Constitution, as under the Confederation.

This Constitution, and the Laws of the United States which shall be made in Pursuance thereof; and all Treaties made, or which shall be made, under the Authority of the United States, shall be the supreme Law of the Land; and the Judges in every State shall be bound thereby, any Thing in the Constitution or Laws of any State to the Contrary notwithstanding.

The Senators and Representatives before mentioned, and the Members of the several State Legislatures, and all executive and judicial Officers, both of the United States and of the several States, shall be bound by Oath or Affirmation, to support this Constitution; but no religious Test shall ever be required as a Qualification to any Office or public Trust under the United States.

Article. VII.

The Ratification of the Conventions of nine States, shall be sufficient for the Establishment of this Constitution between the States so ratifying the Same.

Done in Convention by the Unanimous Consent of the States present the Seventeenth Day of September in the Year of our Lord one thousand seven hundred and Eighty seven and of the Independence of the United States of America the Twelfth In Witness whereof We have hereunto subscribed our Names,

Go. Washington–Presidt.
and deputy from Virginia

NEW HAMPSHIRE

John Langdon
Nicholas Gilman

MASSACHUSETTS

Nathaniel Gorham
Rufus King

CONNECTICUT

Wm. Saml. Johnson
Roger Sherman

NEW YORK

Alexander Hamilton

NEW JERSEY

Wil: Livingston
David Brearley
Wm. Paterson
Jona: Dayton

PENNSYLVANIA

B Franklin
Thomas Mifflin
Robt Morris
Geo. Clymer
Thos. FitzSimons
Jared Ingersoll
James Wilson
Gouv Morris

DELAWARE

  Geo. Read
  Gunning Bedford Jun
  John Dickinson
  Richard Bassett
  Jaco. Broom

MARYLAND

  James McHenry
  Dan of St. Thos. Jenifer
  Danl Carroll

VIRGINIA

  John Blair
  James Madison Jr.

NORTH CAROLINA

  Wm. Blount
  Richd. Dobbs Spaight
  Hu Williamson

SOUTH CAROLINA

  J. Rutledge
  Charles Cotesworth Pinckney
  Charles Pinckney
  Pierce Butler

GEORGIA

  William Few
  Abr Baldwin

Attest William Jackson Secretary

In Convention Monday
September 17th, 1787
Present
The States of
New Hampshire, Massachusetts, Connecticut, Mr. Hamilton from New York, New Jersey, Pennsylvania, Delaware, Maryland, Virginia, North Carolina, South Carolina and Georgia.

Resolved,
That the preceeding Constitution be laid before the United States in Congress assembled, and that it is the Opinion of this Convention, that it should afterwards be submitted to a Convention of Delegates, chosen in each State by the People thereof, under the Recommendation of its Legislature, for their Assent and Ratification; and that each Convention assenting to, and ratifying the Same, should give Notice thereof to the United States in Congress assembled. Resolved, That it is the Opinion of this Convention, that as soon as the Conventions of nine States shall have ratified this Constitution, the United States in Congress assembled should fix a Day on which Electors should be appointed by the States which shall have ratified the same, and a Day on which the Electors should assemble to vote for the President, and the Time and Place for commencing Proceedings under this Constitution.

That after such Publication the Electors should be appointed, and the Senators and Representatives elected; That the Electors should meet on the Day fixed for the Election of the President, and should transmit their Votes certified, signed, sealed and directed, as the Constitution requires, to the Secretary of the United States in Congress assembled, that the Senators and Representatives should convene at the Time and Place assigned; that the Senators should appoint a President of the Senate, for the sole Purpose of receiving, opening and counting the Votes for President; and, that after he shall be chosen, the Congress, together with the President, should, without Delay, proceed to execute this Constitution.

By the unanimous Order of the Convention

Go. Washington Presidt.
W. JACKSON Secretary

* Language in brackets has been changed by amendment

CONSTITUTION OF THE UNITED STATES

James Pace

THE AMENDMENTS TO THE CONSTITUTION OF THE UNITED STATES AS RATIFIED BY THE STATES

Preamble to the Bill of Rights

Congress of the United States
begun and held at the City of New York, on
Wednesday the fourth of March,

THE Conventions of a number of the States, having at the time of their adopting the Constitution, expressed a desire, in order to prevent misconstruction or abuse of its powers, that further declaratory and restrictive clauses should be added: And as extending the ground of public confidence in the Government, will best ensure the beneficent ends of its institution

RESOLVED by the Senate and House of Representatives of the United States of America, in Congress assembled, two thirds of both Houses concurring, that the following Articles be proposed to the Legislatures of the several States, as amendments to the Constitution of the United States; all, or any of which Articles, when ratified by three fourths of the said Legislatures, to be valid to all intents and purposes, as part of the said Constitution; viz.

ARTICLES in addition to, and Amendment of the Constitution of the United States of America, proposed by Congress, and ratified by the Legislatures of the several States, pursuant to the fifth Article of the original Constitution.

(Note: The first 10 amendments to the Constitution were ratified December 15, 1791, and form what is known as the "Bill of Rights.")

Amendment I.

Congress shall make no law respecting an establishment of religion, or prohibiting the free exercise thereof; or abridging the freedom of speech, or of the press; or the right of the people peaceably to assemble, and to petition the Government for a redress of grievances.

Amendment II.

A well regulated Militia, being necessary to the security of a free State, the right of the people to keep and bear Arms, shall not be infringed.

Amendment III.

No Soldier shall, in time of peace be quartered in any house, without the consent of the Owner, nor in time of war, but in a manner to be prescribed by law.

Amendment IV.

The right of the people to be secure in their persons, houses, papers, and effects, against unreasonable searches and seizures, shall not be violated, and no Warrants shall issue, but upon probable cause, supported by Oath or affirmation, and particularly describing the place to be searched, and the persons or things to be seized.

Amendment V.

No person shall be held to answer for a capital, or otherwise infamous crime, unless on a presentment or indictment of a Grand Jury, except in cases arising in the land or naval forces, or in the Militia, when in actual service in time of War or public danger; nor shall any person be subject for the same offence to be twice put in jeopardy of life or limb; nor shall be compelled in any criminal case to be a witness against himself, nor be deprived of life, liberty, or property, without due process of law; nor shall private property be taken for public use, without just compensation.

The ultimate BLONDE joke book and other fun stuff

Amendment VI.

In all criminal prosecutions, the accused shall enjoy the right to a speedy and public trial, by an impartial jury of the State and district wherein the crime shall have been committed, which district shall have been previously ascertained by law, and to be informed of the nature and cause of the accusation; to be confronted with the witnesses against him; to have compulsory process for obtaining witnesses in his favor, and to have the Assistance of Counsel for his defence.

Amendment VII.

In suits at common law, where the value in controversy shall exceed twenty dollars, the right of trial by jury shall be preserved, and no fact tried by a jury, shall be otherwise re-examined in any Court of the United States, than according to the rules of the common law.

Amendment VIII.

Excessive bail shall not be required, nor excessive fines imposed, nor cruel and unusual punishments inflicted.

Amendment IX.

The enumeration in the Constitution, of certain rights, shall not be construed to deny or disparage others retained by the people.

Amendment X.

The powers not delegated to the United States by the Constitution, nor prohibited by it to the States, are reserved to the States respectively, or to the people.

AMENDMENTS 11-27

Amendment XI.

Passed by Congress March 4, 1794. Ratified February 7, 1795.

(Note: Article III, Section 2 of the Constitution was modified by the 11th Amendment.)

The Judicial power of the United States shall not be construed to extend to any suit in law or equity, commenced or prosecuted against one of the United States by Citizens of another State, or by Citizens or Subjects of any Foreign State.

Amendment XII.

Passed by Congress December 9, 1803. Ratified June 15, 1804.

(Note: A portion of Article II, Section 1 of the Constitution was changed by the 12th Amendment.)

The Electors shall meet in their respective states, and vote by ballot for President and Vice-President, one of whom, at least, shall not be an inhabitant of the same state with themselves; they shall name in their ballots the person voted for as President, and in distinct ballots the person voted for as Vice-President, and they shall make distinct lists of all persons voted for as President, and of all persons voted for as Vice-President, and of the number of votes for each, which lists they shall sign and certify, and transmit sealed to the seat of the government of the United States, directed to the President of the Senate; the President of the Senate shall, in the presence of the Senate and House of Representatives, open all the certificates and the votes shall then be counted; The person having the greatest number of votes for President, shall be the President, if such number be a majority of the whole number of Electors appointed; and if no person have such majority, then from the persons having the highest numbers not exceeding three on the list of those voted for as President, the House of Representatives shall choose immediately, by ballot, the President. But in choosing the President, the votes shall be taken by states, the representation from each state having one vote; a quorum for this purpose shall consist of a member or members from two-thirds of the states, and a majority of all the states shall be necessary to a choice. [And if the House of Representatives shall not choose a President whenever the right of choice shall devolve upon them, before the fourth day of March next following, then the Vice-President shall act as President, as in case of the death or other constitutional disability of the President.]* The person having the greatest number of votes as Vice-President, shall be the Vice-President, if such number be a majority of the whole number of Electors appointed, and if no person have a majority, then from the two highest numbers on the list, the Senate shall choose the Vice-President; a quorum for the purpose shall consist of two-thirds of the whole number of Senators, and a majority of the whole number shall be necessary to a choice. But no person constitutionally ineligible to the office of President shall be eligible to that of Vice-President of the United States.

*Superseded by Section 3 of the 20th Amendment.

Amendment XIII.

Passed by Congress January 31, 1865. Ratified December 6, 1865.

(Note: A portion of Article IV, Section 2 of the Constitution was changed by the 13th Amendment.)

SECTION 1

Neither slavery nor involuntary servitude, except as a punishment for crime whereof the party shall have been duly convicted, shall exist within the United States, or any place subject to their jurisdiction.

SECTION 2

Congress shall have power to enforce this article by appropriate legislation.

Amendment XIV.

Passed by Congress June 13, 1866. Ratified July 9, 1868.

(Note: Article I, Section 2 of the Constitution was modified by Section 2 of the 14th Amendment.)

SECTION 1

All persons born or naturalized in the United States and subject to the jurisdiction thereof, are citizens of the United States and of the State wherein they reside. No State shall make or enforce any law which shall abridge the privileges or immunities of citizens of the United States; nor shall any State deprive any person of life, liberty, or property, without due process of law; nor deny to any person within its jurisdiction the equal protection of the laws.

SECTION 2

Representatives shall be apportioned among the several States according to their respective numbers, counting the whole number of persons in each State, excluding Indians not taxed. But when the right to vote at any election for the choice of electors for President and Vice President of the United States, Representatives in Congress, the Executive and Judicial officers of a State, or the members of the Legislature thereof, is denied to any of the male inhabitants of such State, [being twenty-one years of age,]* and citizens of the United States, or in any way abridged, except for participation in rebellion, or other crime, the basis of representation therein shall be reduced in the proportion which the number of such male citizens shall bear to the whole number of male citizens twenty-one years of age in such State.

SECTION 3

No person shall be a Senator or Representative in Congress, or elector of President and Vice President, or hold any office, civil or military, under the United States, or under any State, who, having previously taken an oath, as a member of Congress, or as an officer of the United States, or as a member of any State legislature, or as an executive or judicial officer of any State, to support the Constitution of the United States, shall have engaged in insurrection or rebellion against the same, or given aid or comfort to the enemies thereof. But Congress may by a vote of two-thirds of each House, remove such disability.

SECTION 4

The validity of the public debt of the United States, authorized by law, including debts incurred for payment of pensions and bounties for services in suppressing insurrection or rebellion, shall not be questioned. But neither the United States nor any State shall assume or pay any debt or obligation incurred in aid of insurrection or rebellion against the United States, or any claim for the loss or emancipation of any slave; but all such debts, obligations and claims shall be held illegal and void.

SECTION 5

The Congress shall have the power to enforce, by appropriate legislation, the provisions of this article.

*Changed by Section 1 of the 26th Amendment.

Amendment XV.

Passed by Congress February 26, 1869. Ratified February 3, 1870.

SECTION 1

The right of citizens of the United States to vote shall not be denied or abridged by the United States or by any State on account of race, color, or previous condition of servitude.

SECTION 2

The Congress shall have the power to enforce this article by appropriate legislation.

Amendment XVI.

Passed by Congress July 2, 1909. Ratified February 3, 1913.

(Note: Article I, Section 9 of the Constitution was modified by the 16th Amendment.)

The Congress shall have power to lay and collect taxes on incomes, from whatever source derived, without apportionment among the several States, and without regard to any census or enumeration.

Amendment XVII.

Passed by Congress May 13, 1912. Ratified April 8, 1913.

(Note: Article I, Section 3 of the Constitution was modified by the 17th Amendment.)

The Senate of the United States shall be composed of two Senators from each State, elected by the people thereof, for six years, and each Senator shall have one vote. The electors in each State shall have the qualifications requisite for electors of the most numerous branch of the State legislatures.

When vacancies happen in the representation of any State in the Senate, the executive authority of such State shall issue writs of election to fill such vacancies: Provided, That the legislature of any State may empower the executive thereof to make temporary appointments until the people fill the vacancies by election as the legislature may direct.

This amendment shall not be so construed as to affect the election or term of any Senator chosen before it becomes valid as part of the Constitution.

Amendment XVIII.

Passed by Congress December 18, 1917. Ratified January 16, 1919. Repealed by the 21 Amendment, December 5, 1933.

SECTION 1

After one year from the ratification of this article the manufacture, sale, or transportation of intoxicating liquors within, the importation thereof into, or the exportation thereof from the United States and all territory subject to the jurisdiction thereof for beverage purposes is hereby prohibited.

SECTION 2

The Congress and the several States shall have concurrent power to enforce this article by appropriate legislation.

SECTION 3

This article shall be inoperative unless it shall have been ratified as an amendment to the Constitution by the legislatures of the several States, as provided in the Constitution, within seven years from the date of the submission hereof to the States by the Congress.

Amendment XIX.

Passed by Congress June 4, 1919. Ratified August 18, 1920.

The right of citizens of the United States to vote shall not be denied or abridged by the United States or by any State on account of sex.

Congress shall have power to enforce this article by appropriate legislation.

CONSTITUTION OF THE UNITED STATES

Amendment XX.

Passed by Congress March 2, 1932. Ratified January 23, 1933.

(Note: Article I, Section 4 of the Constitution was modified by Section 2 of this Amendment. In addition, a portion of the 12th Amendment was superseded by Section 3.)

SECTION 1

The terms of the President and the Vice President shall end at noon on the 20th day of January, and the terms of Senators and Representatives at noon on the 3d day of January, of the years in which such terms would have ended if this article had not been ratified; and the terms of their successors shall then begin.

SECTION 2

The Congress shall assemble at least once in every year, and such meeting shall begin at noon on the 3d day of January, unless they shall by law appoint a different day.

SECTION 3

If, at the time fixed for the beginning of the term of the President, the President elect shall have died, the Vice President elect shall become President. If a President shall not have been chosen before the time fixed for the beginning of his term, or if the President elect shall have failed to qualify, then the Vice President elect shall act as President until a President shall have qualified; and the Congress may by law provide for the case wherein neither a President elect nor a Vice President elect shall have qualified, declaring who shall then act as President, or the manner in which one who is to act shall be selected, and such person shall act accordingly until a President or Vice President shall have qualified.

SECTION 4

The Congress may by law provide for the case of the death of any of the persons from whom the House of Representatives may choose a President whenever the right of choice shall have devolved upon them, and for the case of the death of any of the persons from whom the Senate may choose a Vice President whenever the right of choice shall have devolved upon them.

SECTION 5

Sections 1 and 2 shall take effect on the 15th day of October following the ratification of this article.

SECTION 6

This article shall be inoperative unless it shall have been ratified as an amendment to the Constitution by the legislatures of three-fourths of the several States within seven years from the date of its submission.

Amendment XXI.

Passed by Congress February 20, 1933. Ratified December 5, 1933.

SECTION 1

The eighteenth article of amendment to the Constitution of the United States is hereby repealed.

SECTION 2

The transportation or importation into any State, Territory, or possession of the United States for delivery or use therein of intoxicating liquors, in violation of the laws thereof, is hereby prohibited.

SECTION 3

This article shall be inoperative unless it shall have been ratified as an amendment to the Constitution by conventions in the several States, as provided in the Constitution, within seven years from the date of the submission hereof to the States by the Congress.

Amendment XXII.

Passed by Congress March 21, 1947. Ratified February 27, 1951.

SECTION 1

No person shall be elected to the office of the President more than twice, and no person who has held the office of President, or acted as President, for more than two years of a term to which some other person was elected President shall be elected to the office of President more than once. But this Article shall not apply to any person holding the office of President when this Article was proposed by Congress, and shall not prevent any person who may be holding the office of President, or acting as President, during the term within which this Article becomes operative from holding the office of President or acting as President during the remainder of such term.

SECTION 2

This article shall be inoperative unless it shall have been ratified as an amendment to the Constitution by the legislatures of three-fourths of the several States within seven years from the date of its submission to the States by the Congress.

Amendment XXIII.

Passed by Congress June 16, 1960. Ratified March 29, 1961.

SECTION 1

The District constituting the seat of Government of the United States shall appoint in such manner as Congress may direct:

A number of electors of President and Vice President equal to the whole number of Senators and Representatives in Congress to which the District would be entitled if it were a State, but in no event more than the least populous State; they shall be in addition to those appointed by the States, but they shall be considered, for the purposes of the election of President and Vice President, to be electors appointed by a State; and they shall meet in the District and perform such duties as provided by the twelfth article of amendments.

SECTION 2

The Congress shall have power to enforce this article by appropriate legislation.

Amendment XXIV.

Passed by Congress August 27, 1962. Ratified January 23, 1964.

SECTION 1

The right of citizens of the United States to vote in any primary or other election for President or Vice President, for electors for President or Vice President, or for Senator or Representative in Congress, shall not be denied or abridged by the United States or any State by reason of failure to pay poll tax or other tax.

SECTION 2

The Congress shall have power to enforce this article by appropriate legislation.

CONSTITUTION OF THE UNITED STATES

Amendment XXV.

Passed by Congress July 6, 1965. Ratified February 10, 1967.

(Note: Article II, Section 1 of the Constitution was modified by the 25th Amendment.)

SECTION 1

In case of the removal of the President from office or of his death or resignation, the Vice President shall become President.

SECTION 2

Whenever there is a vacancy in the office of the Vice President, the President shall nominate a Vice President who shall take office upon confirmation by a majority vote of both Houses of Congress.

SECTION 3

Whenever the President transmits to the President pro tempore of the Senate and the Speaker of the House of Representatives his written declaration that he is unable to discharge the powers and duties of his office, and until he transmits to them a written declaration to the contrary, such powers and duties shall be discharged by the Vice President as Acting President.

SECTION 4

Whenever the Vice President and a majority of either the principal officers of the executive departments or of such other body as Congress may by law provide, transmit to the President pro tempore of the Senate and the Speaker of the House of Representatives their written declaration that the President is unable to discharge the powers and duties of his office, the Vice President shall immediately assume the powers and duties of the office as Acting President.

Thereafter, when the President transmits to the President pro tempore of the Senate and the Speaker of the House of Representatives his written declaration that no inability exists, he shall resume the powers and duties of his office unless the Vice President and a majority of either the principal officers of the executive department or of such other body as Congress may by law provide, transmit within four days to the President pro tempore of the Senate and the Speaker of the House of Representatives their written declaration that the President is unable to discharge the powers and duties of his office. Thereupon Congress shall decide the issue, assembling within forty-eight hours for that purpose if not in session. If the Congress, within twenty-one days after receipt of the latter written declaration, or, if Congress is not in session, within twenty-one days after Congress is required to assemble, determines by two thirds vote of both Houses that the President is unable to discharge the powers and duties of his office, the Vice President shall continue to discharge the same as Acting President; otherwise, the President shall resume the powers and duties of his office.

Amendment XXVI.

Passed by Congress March 23, 1971. Ratified July 1, 1971.

(Note: Amendment 14, Section 2 of the Constitution was modified by Section 1 of the 26th Amendment.)

SECTION 1

The right of citizens of the United States, who are eighteen years of age or older, to vote shall not be denied or abridged by the United States or by any State on account of age.

SECTION 2

The Congress shall have power to enforce this article by appropriate legislation.

Amendment XXVII.

Originally proposed Sept. 25, 1789. Ratified May 7, 1992.

No law, varying the compensation for the services of the Senators and Representatives, shall take effect, until an election of representatives shall have intervened.

Patriotic Songs

"The Star Spangled Banner"

Francis Scott Key (1814)

Oh, say, can you see, by the dawn's early light, What so proudly we hail'd at the twilight's last gleaming? Whose broad stripes and bright stars, thro' the perilous fight, O'er the ramparts we watch'd, were so gallantly streaming? And the rockets' red glare, the bombs bursting in air, Gave proof thro' the night that our flag was still there. O say, does that star-spangled banner yet wave O'er the land of the free and the home of the brave?

Pledge of Allegiance

by Captain George Thatcher Balch 1885

I pledge allegiance To the flag Of the United States of America And to the republic For which it stands One Nation under God, Indivisible, With liberty and justice for

Battle Hymn of the Republic

by Julia Ward Howe

Published 1861

[Verse & Chorus 1]

Mine eyes have seen the glory of the coming of the Lord;

He is trampling out the vintage where the grapes
of wrath are stored;

He hath loosed the fateful lightning of His terrible
swift sword;

His truth is marching on.

Glory! Glory! Hallelujah! Glory! Glory! Hallelujah!

Glory! Glory! Hallelujah! His truth is marching on.

[Verse & Chorus 2]

I have seen Him in the watch fires of a hundred
circling camps

They have builded Him an altar in the evening
dews and damps;

I can read His righteous sentence by the dim and
flaring lamps;

His day is marching on.

Glory! Glory! Hallelujah! Glory! Glory! Hallelujah!

Glory! Glory! Hallelujah! His day is marching on.

[Verse & Chorus 3]

I have read a fiery Gospel writ in burnished rows
of steel;

"As ye deal with My contemners, so with you My
grace shall deal";

Let the Hero, born of woman, crush the serpent
with His heel,

Since God is marching on.

Glory! Glory! Hallelujah! Glory! Glory! Hallelujah!

Glory! Glory! Hallelujah! Since God is marching on.

[Verse & Chorus 4]

He has sounded forth the trumpet that shall never call retreat;

He is sifting out the hearts of men before His judgment seat;

Oh, be swift, my soul, to answer Him! be jubilant, my feet;

Our God is marching on.

Glory! Glory! Hallelujah! Glory! Glory! Hallelujah!

Glory! Glory! Hallelujah! Our God is marching on.

[Verse & Chorus 5]

In the beauty of the lilies Christ was born across the sea,

With a glory in His bosom that transfigures you and me:

As He died to make men holy, let us live to make men free;

[originally …let us die to make men free]

While God is marching on.

Glory! Glory! Hallelujah! Glory! Glory! Hallelujah!

Glory! Glory! Hallelujah! While God is marching on.

[Verse & Chorus 6]

He is coming like the glory of the morning on the wave,

He is wisdom to the mighty, He is honor to the brave;

So the world shall be His footstool, and the soul of wrong His slave,

Our God is marching on.

Glory! Glory! Hallelujah! Glory! Glory! Hallelujah!

Glory! Glory! Hallelujah! Our God is marching on.CHORUS

The Liberty Song (1768)

by John Dickinson

Chorus

"Come, join hand in hand, brave Americans all
And rouse your bold hearts at fair Liberty's call.
No tyrannous acts shall suppress your just claim
Or stain with dishonor America's name.

Chorus

In freedom we're born and in freedom we'll live.
Our purses are ready. Steady, boys, steady.
Not as slaves but as Freemen our money we'll give.
Our worthy forefathers, let's give them a cheer
To climates unknown did courageously steer.
Through oceans to deserts for freedom they came
And dying, bequeath'd us their freedom and fame.

Chorus

The tree their own hands had to Liberty reared
They lived to behold growing strong and revered.
With transport they cried, now our wishes we gain
For our children shall gather the fruits of our pain.

Chorus

Then join hand in hand, brave Americans all

By uniting we stand, by dividing we fall

In so righteous a cause let us hope to succeed
For heaven approves of each generous deed.

Chorus

This Land Is Your Land

by Woody Guthrie 1956

This land is your land, and this land is my land
From California to the New York island
From the Redwood Forest to the Gulf Stream waters
This land was made for you and me

As I went walking that ribbon of highway

And I saw above me that endless skyway

I saw below me that golden valley

This land was made for you and me

I roamed and rambled, and I've followed my footsteps

To the sparkling sands of her diamond deserts

All around me, a voice was sounding

This land was made for you and me

There was a big, high wall there that tried to stop me

A sign was painted said "Private Property"

But on the backside, it didn't say nothing

This land was made for you and me

When the sun come shining, then I was strolling

And the wheat fields waving, and the dust clouds rolling

The voice was chanting as the fog was lifting

This land was made for you and me

This land is your land, and this land is my land

From California to the New York island

From the Redwood Forest to the Gulf Stream waters

This land was made for you and me

My country, 'tis of thee
By S.F. Smith 1831

My country, 'tis of thee,
Sweet land of liberty,
Of thee I sing;
Land where my fathers died,
Land of the Pilgrims' Pride,
From every mountain side
Let freedom ring.

My native country, thee,
Land of the noble, free,
Thy name I love;
I love thy rocks and rills,
Thy woods and templed hills,
My heart with rapture thrills,
Like that above.

Let music swell the breeze,
And ring from all the trees
Sweet freedom's song;
Let mortal tongues awake,

Let all that breathe partake,
Let rocks their silence break,
The sound prolong.

Our fathers' God, to Thee,
Author of liberty,
To Thee we sing;
Long may our land be bright,
With freedom's holy light,
Protect us by Thy might,
Great God, our King.

Autographs

Notes

The ultimate BLONDE joke book and other fun stuff

Made in the USA
Columbia, SC
06 January 2025